PEOPLE

For Vanessa Contessa, my pride and joy.

Assouline Publishing, Inc.
601 West 26th Street
18th floor
New York, NY 10001
USA
www.assouline.com

Text by Vanessa C. Salle
Photo editing: Jesse Frohman

ISBN: 2 84323 286 4

Printed in Italy

ROXANNE LOWIT

PEOPLE

ASSOULINE

introduction

My life is filled with the fabulous and the glamorous: people, parties, fashion, models, celebrities, drag queens—but it didn't start out that way. As a child, I loved to draw and paint. It was very rewarding. Later, as I learned more of the world at large, I discovered modern art and was inspired by artists like Matisse and Picasso and the pioneers of modern art who introduced a new way of perception; whose contributions to society by sharing their vision made the world sit up and take notice. Think deeper and feel more. So when the time came, I sent myself to a good art school in New York City to study art and fashion and to learn a trade. I graduated from the Fashion Institute of Technology with a degree in textile designing, specializing in hand screen printing and worked for many years at one of the best firms in New York City, as their head designer.

Then, one fateful day, someone gave me a little instamatic camera. I took pictures of everything: my daughter, my life, photos of friends whose portraits I wanted to paint—but who had time to sit for a portrait? Soon I realized that I didn't need to paint the portraits at all because I had found a vehicle as malleable and expressive as the brush. Photography satisfied my need for instant gratification as well, for I am of the culture of fast food and fast cars.

The camera allows me to capture something beyond what is seen by the naked eye. The camera became an obsession, as well as a source of pleasure. I was constantly shooting the people, the models, the designers, the fashion, the parties: whatever intrigued me. Mostly it was just for me, for fun. The more photos I took, the more I loved taking photos (and the less I liked designing). From the beginning, I seemed to have an affinity for photography.

Twenty-five years ago, I received an offer I couldn't refuse. Annie Flanders of the *SoHo News*, who had come over to look at my work, said that if I were to get a professional camera and shoot the shows in Paris, she would run my photos in the paper. The next thing I knew, I was on a plane to Paris reading the instructions on how to load the film for my new camera.

I covered the shows from backstage. The models snuck me in as their hairdresser. The photos ran on the cover of the *SoHo News*, a few pages on the inside and as the poster advertising the issue. It doubled the circulation of the paper. I thought, "This is fun and easy!"

Backstage stirs my passion to capture moments and people—sometimes waiting for things to happen naturally and other times creating a moment of my own. One can find lots of energy, excitement, sometimes even a bit of drama. Today the media takes the world for a peek "behind the scenes"; twenty-five years ago, no one else was interested in providing an intimate look into the world of fashion and showing a side of nightlife that most people did not get to see.

My photos ran in the *SoHo News* and I decided to become a full-time photographer. Everyone thought that I was crazy leaving my secure and steady job as a designer. But I just loved taking pictures. It was so rewarding that I just had to take a chance. I was amazed to suddenly find my work within the pages of a succession of magazines including *The New York Times*, Italian *Vogue*, American *Vogue*, *Vanity*, *Vanity Fair*, and *Allure*, to name a few.

The rest is, as the saying goes, history. My passion had become my métier. I realize that I am a voyeur. I get to walk through amazing lives, meeting incredible, interesting people on the way and have the opportunity to go to the most extraordinary parties and fashion shows, and all for work. It is a great pleasure.

My camera is like an extension of my arm, as a sword is to a samurai, always with me, allowing me to freeze time, seizing up an era or an instant. I enjoy every aspect of my work, from going into the enchanting world of stunning designs, glamorous settings and beautiful people, retrieving my own perceptions as they emerge from the printing solution, to the time it appears in the pages of a magazine or framed on a wall.

My vocation has provided me with an education. What have I learned? A non-judgmental empathy, and a recognition of the flexibility of reality—positions can change as well as perceptions. The quality of fashion is fascinating—it mandates both conformity and change. As with the click of a shutter—timing is everything!

Previously there was more life then art, and art was valued for its capacity to imitate life. Today life is filled with popular art and we mimic what happens on the many screens we watch that come between us and life. We put on our values as if they were clothes. We wear less clothes—and how we wear them is supposed to indicate who we really are.

An artist friend once told me that Surrealism was defined as finding the strange in the everyday. He said that in my work I managed to find what Fellini missed—the surreal in the strange. I feel privileged to be able to record this era of recent history. After all, art and fashion are regarded by historians to be a living record of a culture and an era. I hope to have done my part in helping to record the expression of value and taste.

The journey to that end has been personally pleasurable and vitally fulfilling.

the woman who believes in magic

I asked Roxanne Lowit, who took all the pictures in this book, what it is that she thinks connects all of the people who are in it. She replied, "They're people who fascinate me—people with magic." Her comment is especially telling when one considers what is going on in this book—something that makes it immediately different from so many other celebrity books.

Photography is often considered the second-class citizen of the arts—their servant, as it were. Not here. There's a photographer—David LaChapelle—on the cover, cavorting in the night with Pamela Anderson, and throughout the book images of other photographers are woven amongst the movie stars, pop stars, fashion stars, art stars, and those who Andy Warhol called superstars, when they didn't really have a job other than general fabulousness. In these pages you'll find Lowit's images of all kinds of photographers, such as Warhol, Helmut Newton, Richard Avedon, Mario Testino, Ellen Von Unwerth, Robert Mapplethorpe, and plenty of others. In a way her book is a love letter to photography. In Lowit's pictures the photographers all seem to be having a grand old time. And on page 311 is Lowit's portrait of Bill Cunningham—to me it's a kind of self-portrait of Lowit, as well, because there's something in it which is profoundly true of her too.

While there are big differences in their work, both Lowit and Cunningham shoot out and about on the scene. They are more like street photographers—capturing real life as it happens outside, at parties, and around the fashion world—than they are studio or session photographers. Cunningham's portrait by Lowit is an image taken at night, and even though he's dressed up like a swell, in a tuxedo, one can tell that he is working. His camera is in his hands ready to go at the hint of a potential picture. He has probably been at it for hours, but instead of seeming exhausted he has one of the biggest smiles you've ever seen. If it was the old days when they used to put descriptive captions under the photographs, it would read, "This man loves his work." Lowit is clearly trying to tell us something. And it's about herself and photography too. Indeed when I asked Lowit what it was that drove her around 1977 from her first career in textiles to become a photographer she explained: "I really wanted to love with my heart what I did. I wanted to be excited about my work."

It's almost twenty-five years later, and she still comes across as someone who completely has her heart in her work. Originally Lowit got herself backstage at the fashion shows in Paris and has basically been a behind-the-scenes photographer ever since. When she started out she was an anathema in her profession. As she says, "It was all about big guys with big cameras and a lot of equipment and big bags; in their safari jackets it was like they were going off to war." That wasn't Lowit's style. Hers is way more subtle, more chameleon-like. Dressed in black she always fits in wherever she goes.

When we were talking recently I asked Lowit how she felt about the fact that her type of candid photography tends to get less respect than other kinds of photography do, such as art photography or studio photography, she replied that she's never cared about any of that. She said: "To me there's a challenge about catching people when they're being themselves. Even out in public there is the soul of what is happening. The recording of it and making a really beautiful picture out of it is something that I wanted to do. It's still something that I want to do. I'm a voyeur and I love watching people." You can sense all of this in Lowit's photography. You can also feel the way people trust her. The fantastically alive pictures that she gets, would not happen without that trust.

Knowing how much Roxanne loves the night and all that it brings, and aware of all the unforgettable images she has shot after dark, many of which are included in this book, I asked her if she thought that things had gotten tamer over the years. Here is what she said:

> "Well, I thought they were looser before in the days of Studio 54 when we would dance all night and thought we would live forever. But then I went to Amanda Lepore's birthday party and she was wearing this lovely red dress, and said I had to stay for her performance. Her performance was a strip and then she turned around at the end, and she had a penis. She looked down and screamed. Next Sofia came on stage in high heels and fishnets, no top on, with a big scissor and a flying-nun nurse's hat on. She "cut" the penis off—with fake blood spurting everywhere. Meanwhile the kids at the club, a straight and gay mix, were completely blasé, as if to say oh it's just another performance, just another night. So I guess it's pretty wild out there."

This said, Lowit laughs. It's clear how much affection she has for the people she photographs. Look at her pictures and you'll see warmth and no judgment. You'll also see the work of an inside observer who has a sharp eye for a memorable moment. You'll find the kind of passion for photography that does the medium proud.

ingrid sischy

this is...

When I look at this visual history book that Roxanne has compiled I think: this is why I came to New York. I think, this is why everybody came to New York. And why we went to Paris and London and Milan—all of those other places—and why we came back.

This is why I got a job working for magazines, so I could meet these people and get in the front door, or the back door, or the side door.

When I look at Roxanne's pictures I think, these are like the pictures God would take: you can tell what everyone is thinking.

When I look at Roxanne's pictures it takes me back more than any words ever could. This is time travel. Beam me down, Roxanne.

This was the life; this is the life. But it's not easy.

This is why they printed drink tickets.

This is why I learned the names of all the club doormen.

This is why hundreds of people were standing in front of the place yelling "Mark!" or "Steve!"

This is why I decided that I'd better start getting up before the banks closed if I was ever going to make any money.

This is what Andy called going to work. This is all deductible.

This is why Lou wrote "All Tomorrow's Parties."

This is why you should keep the table in front of you fairly bare at one of those things. They'll look at the picture and think you drank all those drinks and smoked all those cigarettes.

When I look at Roxanne's pictures I think, these are like the pictures Santa Claus would take if he were an artist: she knows when you are sleeping, she knows when you're awake, she knows when you've been bad or good...
This is why I gave up smoking.
This is why they have all those anonymous meetings.
This is why I brush my teeth before going out for the evening and check them again after the meal.
Roxanne gives new meaning to the expression "keep your eye on the ball."
This is why I know everybody in the art world. And the fashion world. And eventually the world.
This is why the next day in the paper they say, "We're just good friends. Sometimes we hold hands."
Roxanne has the eye to have made a great spy, but maybe she is too kind.
This is why there could be a hundred flashes going off, but you know that the definitive shot is Roxanne's.
This is why Andy hated shaking hands: you never know where they've been.
This is why Steve Rubell asked me if I had any coke and I really didn't.
This is why that famous couple broke up. This is why the band broke up.
Roxanne's pictures have no moral but they are a form of judgement: rhythm, frame, seeking the magic. The moral comes later: you get the face you deserve.
This is why hairdressers love Kate Moss.

This is why Halloween doesn't move a real New Yorker.
This is why we took a cab, not the subway.
This is why every man should own a tuxedo. This is why I don't own a wing collar.
These pictures prove that somebody was paying close attention to what was going on and framed things as carefully as Velázquez might have.
This is why they get out of the limo carefully.
This is why it's usually better to eat before the party.
This is why I use my wife's retinol cream before I go to bed at night.
This is why they got the silicon put in and this is why they took it out.
This is why bouncers threw Ricky Clifton through the glass doors.
This is why I woke up on the side of the wrong bed a couple of times.
This is why one bad hair day can haunt you for the rest of your life.
This is why Roxanne is loved, because even when you're doing something naughty, she knows how to make you look good.
This is why they're called supermodels: you remember their name ten years later.
This is why Grace was five hours late.
This separates the phonies from the real phonies.
This will jog the memory of people who were blacked out at the time.
This is why I always specify a famous brand of vodka, even if it's not free.
This is why guys like to go backstage after the fashion show while the models are getting dressed, to congratulate the designer.
In most party pictures the subject is not looking back. Here is the initiated eyeball.

This is how we know we looked younger once.
This shows that it's worth the effort to find unique sunglasses.
This shows that one pose can outlast ten friendships.
This shows that taking a great shot in the middle of a riotous party must be a lot like being a great combat photographer.
This has something to do with designer jeans.
This is why you can't be too careful who you're standing next to at a party.
Most photography is standing around moving lights and arguing over hair, makeup and clothes. With good assistants I could do it. But Roxanne's photography is like shooting skeet.
This is why you see really weird people at the gym.
This is why I know so much about nipples.
This proves it about fashion and victims: some things are worse than being naked.
This proves it, either smile or scowl.
Roxanne's pictures prove what Andy Warhol was trying to tell us:
parties are hard work.
This is all about the bold type.
This is why there are drivers: professional and designated.
This is about keeping your chin up and your eyes open.
This is why the office opens at 10 or 11.
Roxanne's photos demonstrate the truth of the old dictum: history is made at night.

glenn o'brien

about roxanne's people

She seems to be everywhere at the same time. Everywhere means the great continents: America, Europe and Asia. Everywhere means the glowing capitals: New York, London, Paris, Berlin, Tokyo, the centers of fashion and the centers of art, like Venice, Cologne, Düsseldorf and Amsterdam, and who would not know.

Roxanne Lowit has photographed "People," but she has enhanced them to become personalities. Indeed, if her human targets are not stars already, she elevates them to the state of uniqueness, brilliantly focused forever.

There was a classic saying in the Twenties of the last century, when France's Foreign Minister Aristide Briand at the beginning of a political conference said, "Where is Dr. Salomon? [The top photographer at the time.] When he does not photograph us, the public will think that our gathering was not important!"

The same goes for Roxanne Lowit. In fact, she highlights with her photographs a society party, a fashion show, an art vernissage, or any event where luminaries and the culturally of style meet to enjoy extraordinary life and each other. Actually, she rather makes them happen, by ennobling their seconds of appearance into lasting images. Some she has caught by surprise, some just act for her, all seem on top of their vitality, serenity, enjoyment and even exaltation. They all must be pleased to find themselves sorted out for real glamour.

A few of those whom she has immortalized in her first book *Moments* have meanwhile gone to the Gods, such as the incomparable Salvador Dalí. Others could be perceived in their roaring youth. Some are coming back again, matured, and yet in high-spirited poses, all of them radiate the intention to live forever.

And she has even succeeded in achieving the impossible: bringing the three world masters of photography into ONE picture: Richard Avedon, Helmut Newton, and Irving Penn, who usually refuses to have his picture taken, but could not withstand her charm.

Whereas the aggressiveness of the paparazzi is justly being hated, Roxanne's gentle, inconspicuous approach seems to be loved, even longed for. Every subject of her fast attention instinctively knows: this will add to my fame and glory. She floats through the crowd, small, slender, smiling, quickly raising her camera, releasing her shutter at the culmination of a significant passing gesture, always in a friendly spirit, with the chance of flattering.

Thus, she has made friends the world over. She seems to be the darling of prestigious couturiers, renowned artists, fêted society gurus, successful entrepreneurs, and even ordinary folk. She is one with her images, now having brilliantly assembled a new gallery, *People*, who by virtue of her talent are now entering a personal eternity.

Let's face it: Roxanne Lowit is a real sorceress!

Photo specialist, collector, and curator of international exhibitions.
Cologne, June 2001

John Galliano, Paris, 1995.

Debbie Harry, New York, 1981.

Vincent Gallo, Paris, 2000.

Debi Mazar, New York, 1996.

Steven Tyler, New York, 1995.

Rossy De Palma, New York, 1996.

Steve Rubell, Farrah Fawcett, Ryan O'Neal, New York, 1981.

Anthony Kiedis, New York, 1997.

Cab Calloway, New York, 1980.

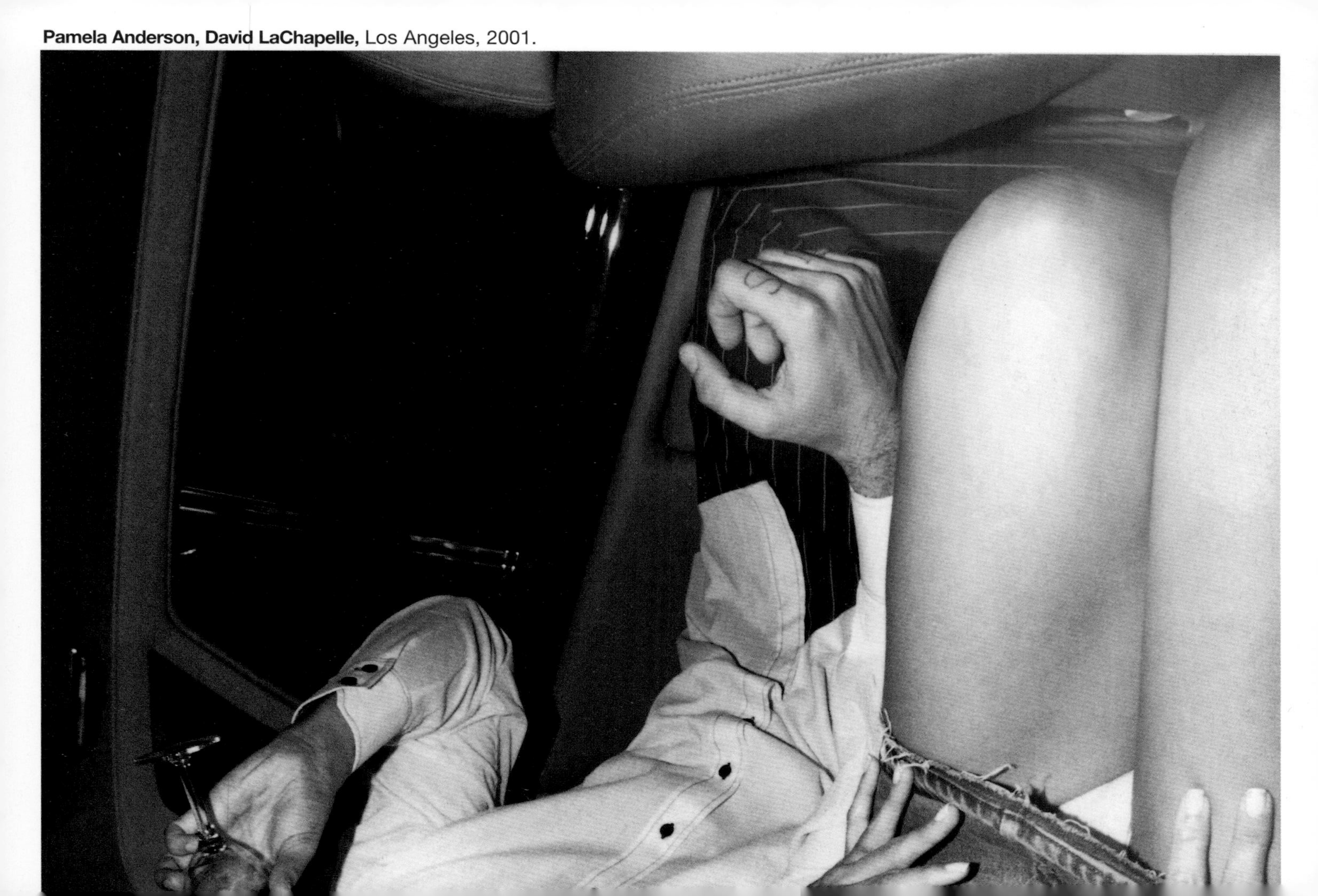

Pamela Anderson, David LaChapelle, Los Angeles, 2001.

Iggy Pop, New York, 1975.

iggy pop

I heard Iggy Pop was going to perform at a small rock 'n' roll club in the East Village, Coney Island High. I thought it would be fun to check him out. I liked him and his music. The stories of his performances were fascinating and stirred my curiosity. When would I have this opportunity again? The club was jam packed! A St. Marks melange of tattooed, pierced punks, computer geeks, a few random folks and me. I made my way up to the front as usual, pushing past the younger fans, to the foot of the stage, front and center. I was so close, I could have reached out and touched him. There I was, bopping my head to the music, when Iggy looked down at me. He nodded at me as if to say hello. I nodded back. He made an expression that said "What are you doing there?" and then gave me an "If you're smart, you'll get out of the way now" look. So I did. As soon as I moved, he took a huge stage dive, and landed right where I would have been standing. It was a thrilling night and now I too have stories about Iggy and his great performances.

Punk Kids, Paris, 1977.

Tara Shannon, Paris, 1979.

David Bowie, New York, 1996.

Camellia Clouse, New York, 1999.

Studio 54, New York, 1979.

Madonna, New York, 1982.

Studio 54, New York, 1978.

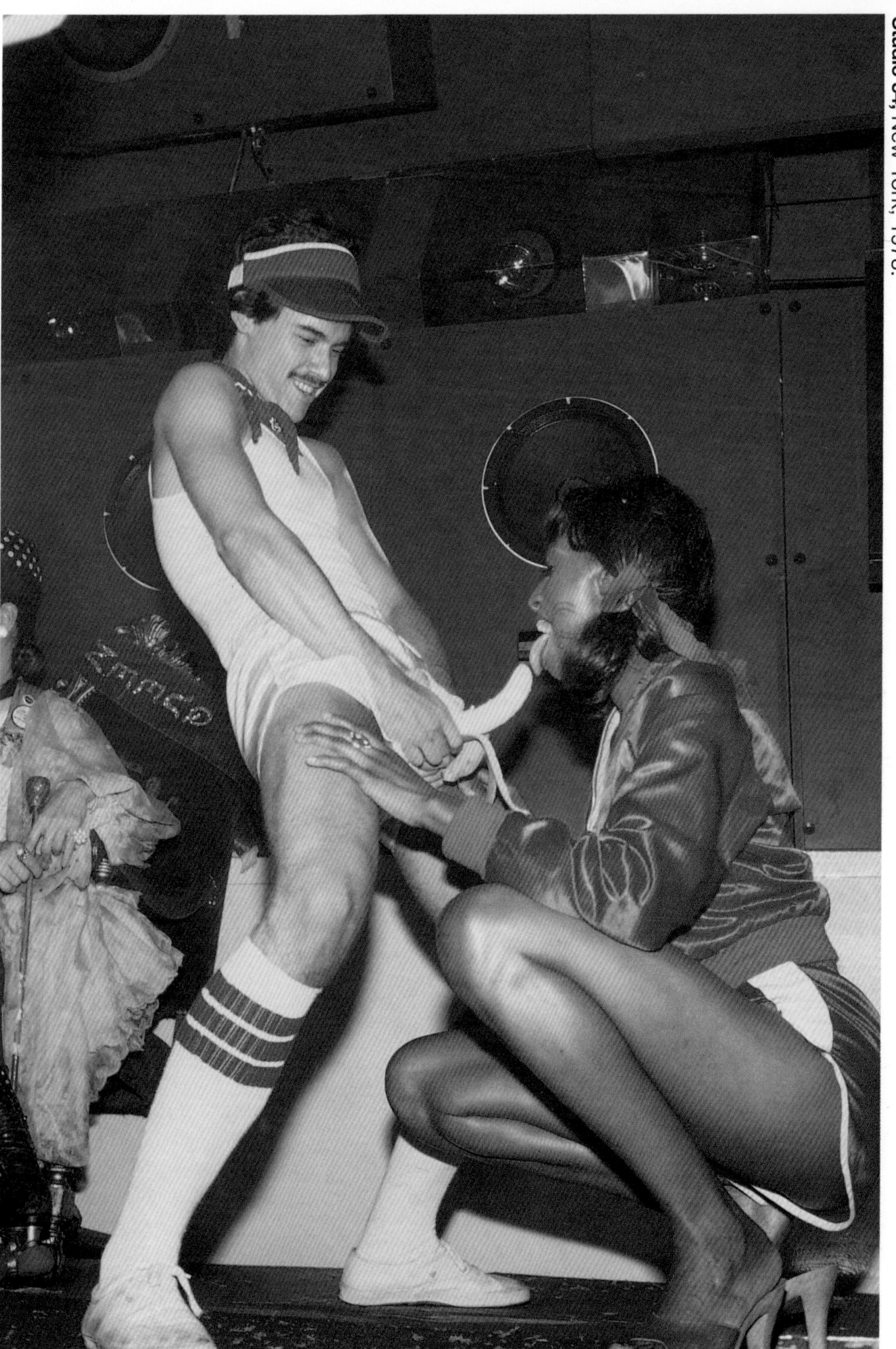

Studio 54, New York, 1978.

Michael Hutchence, Paris, 1992.

Studio 54, New York, 1977.

Ray Charles, New York, 1992.

Chaka Khan, Paris, 1994.

Fayard Nicholas, New York, 1989.

Le Palace, Paris, 1980.

Anne Slater, Foxy Brown, New York, 1997.

foxy brown

I was shooting a star-studded story for *New York Magazine* with people from all walks of life: David Blaine, James King, Alan Cumming, Ute Lemper, Kirsty Hume, Donovan Leitch, Karen Finley, Anne Slater and Foxy Brown were all there. I was shooting smaller groups while waiting for everyone to do the group shot. Foxy Brown still hadn't arrived and she was now a few hours late. Even her personal groomers were waiting for her. She finally arrived but it was still a while before she was ready to join the twelve other people for the shot. After we finished, I thought it would be interesting to shoot Foxy with socialite Anne Slater. Foxy was immediately taken with Anne's exuberant charm and twinkling diamonds. Anne had once told me the story of how her husband proposed to her. I remembered what a delightful story it was and asked her if she would mind sharing the story with Foxy. Her now husband took her out one night to one of their favorite haunts, Le Cirque. He had a pet name for Anne. He liked to call her Mouse. Anne wasn't much of a drinker, but Siro, the owner, told her that he and her beau had invented a new drink that she had to try. It was named after her, the Blue Mouse, because of all her blue glasses which she is still known for. They brought out the drink, a blue that perfectly matched the color of her glasses. It wan't until she was nearly finished that she realized the ice in her drink wasn't ice at all. It was a large diamond engagement ring. We were all mesmerized by the story, especially Foxy. I didn't realize how much of an impression it made on Foxy until almost a year later when I happened to see her latest video in which she is served a blue drink with a big diamond ring in it.

D'Angelo, New York, 1996.

Gloria Gaynor, New York, 1980.

L'il Kim, New York, 1998.

Leroy "Sugar" Bonner, New York, 1996.

Naomi Campbell, New York, 1990.

Al Green, New York, 1989.

Kirsty Hume, Jose Carreño, New York, 1999.

Jean-Michel Basquiat, New York, 1985.

Don King, New York, 1987.

Shalom Harlow, Paris, 1995.

Lenny Kravitz, Iggy Pop, New York, 1998.

Elton John, New York, 1980.

elton john

On Earth Day there was a free concert in Central Park with all sorts of performers. I knew that Elton John was performing and so I worked my way backstage. I don't know how I did it without any credentials. It must have been magic. I simply told anyone who asked that I was there to shoot Elton John. Somehow it worked. Not only did I get backstage, I got on stage. There was Elton in a Donald Duck costume in front of millions of screaming fans and I was there right beside him. If I didn't have the photo to prove it, I might not believe it myself.

Rod Stewart, New York, 1982.

Debbie Harry, Chris Stein, New York, 1989.

Ric Ocasek, New York, 1994.

Paloma Picasso, New York, 1980.

Lou Reed, New York, 1979.

Betsey Johnson, New York, 1977.

Rachel Williams, Los Angeles, 1992.

Robert Mapplethorpe, New York, 1982.

Andy Warhol, Susan Anton, Sylvester Stallone, New York, 1979.

Barney's, New York, 1998.

Diana Ross, New York, 1979.

Jerry Hall, Mick Jagger, New York, 1981.

jerry hall was, and still is, so sexy: tall, blond, slim yet robust and far from ordinary. There was much more than met the eye. Something unmistakably compelling, intoxicating, charming and sweet, with a girlish quality to her—yet undoubtedly all woman. I once covered a lingerie show and Jerry was modeling. When she walked out on to the runway, all the right parts bounced as her long legs strutted down the runway, luxurious hair tossed perfectly this way and that. You could feel the heat rise in the room as the audience roared. hooted and hollered showing their appreciation.

Linda Evangelista, Sylvester Stallone, Paris, 1990.

Johnny Depp, Kate Moss, New York, 1994.

Claude Brouet, Sonia Rykiel, Paris, 1985.

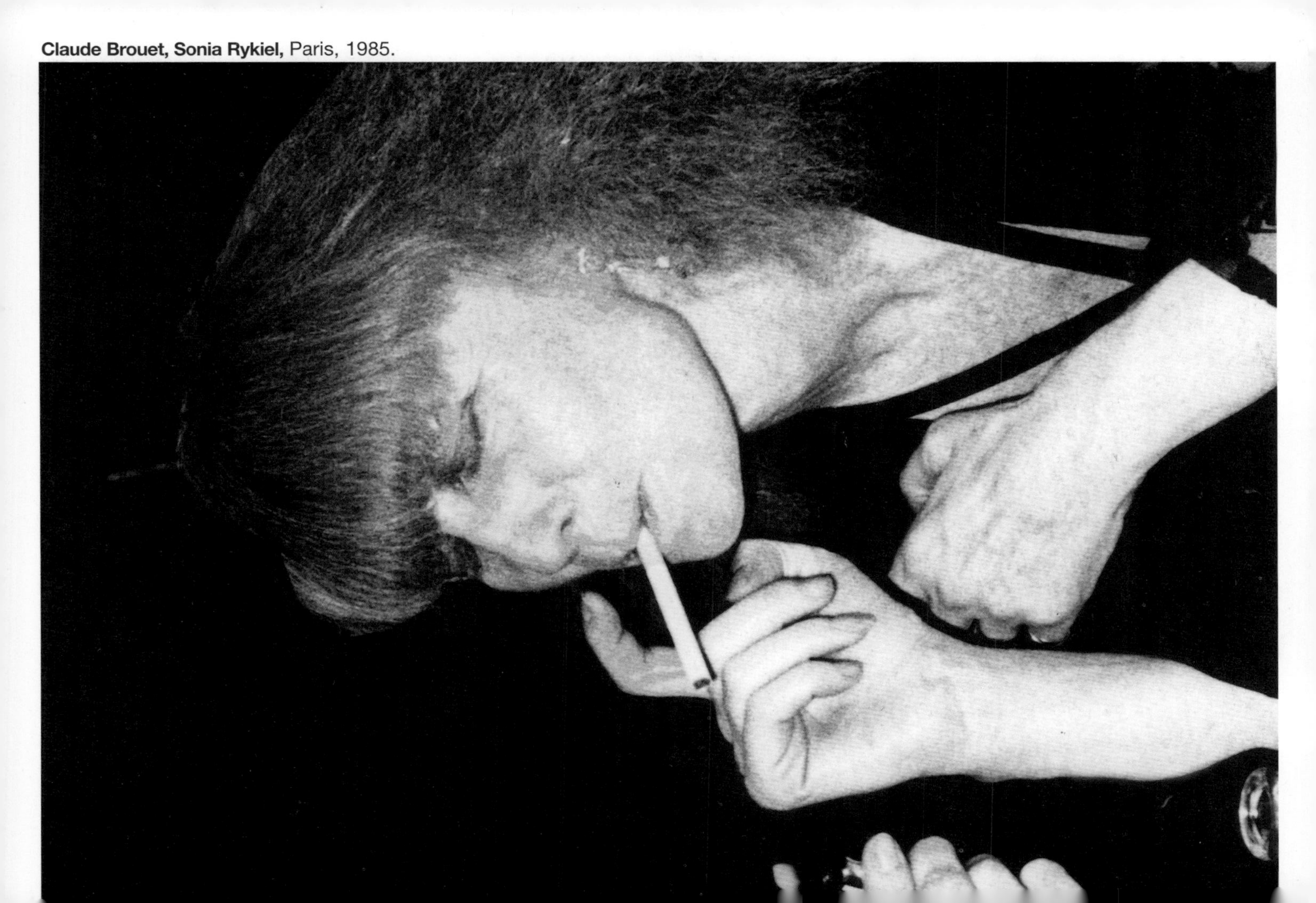

Iman, Paris, 1990.

Grace Jones, New York, 1994.

Julian Schnabel, New York, 2000.

Robert De Niro, New York, 1996.

Leo Castelli, New York, 1992.

Claudia Cardinale, Milan, 1994.

Model and Armen, Los Angeles, 1997.

Sophia Loren, Giorgio Armani, Milan, 1994.

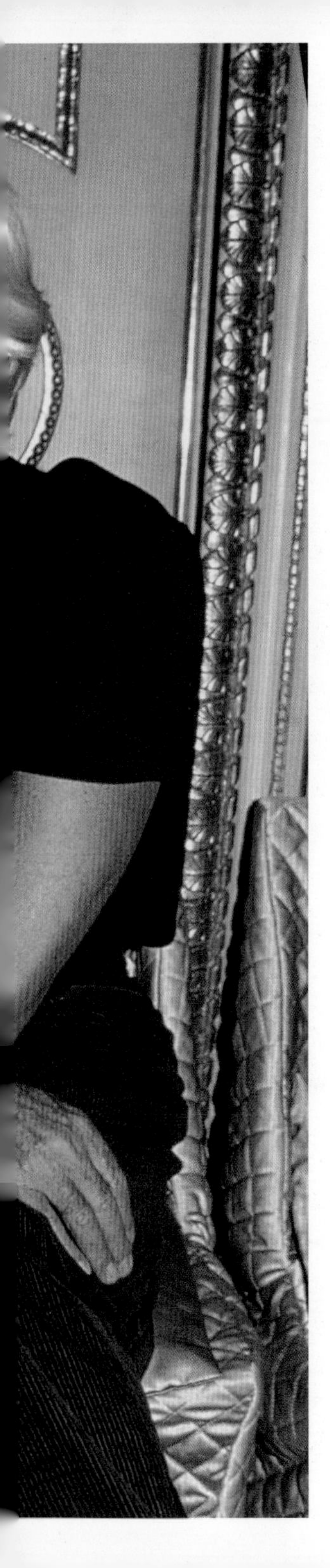

giorgio armani

"A day in the life of Giorgio Armani" was a story I shot for *Vanity Fair* magazine. Mr. Armani was in New York and I had to follow him around and record his every move. He was scheduled to appear on Good Morning America and we had to be there at the crack of dawn—4 a.m., which is closer to the time I usually go to bed, not when I wake up! I remember going to bed the night before, wearing all of my clothes so I would get there on time. When I got there, I was greeted with a smiling, bubbly, charming, chipper Giorgio. He was on! For my cameras as well as for the TV crews, posing, smiling, telling jokes. "Giorgio! I had no idea you were such a ham," I said in French. "Qu'est-ce que c'est, ham?" he asked. I thought for a minute and replied: "Jambon." He laughed and said in Italian: "YOU are calling ME a prosciutto!"

Rudolph Nureyev, Paris, 1989.

Countess Maya Von Schönburg, Paris, 1989.

Pauline Lafont, Paris, 1981.

Inès Sastre, Paris, 2000.

Marc Jacobs, New York, 1989.

John Waters, New York, 1979.

Salma Hayek, New York, 1997.

Antonio Banderas, New York, 1996.

Linda Evangelista, Naomi Campbell, Christy Turlington, New York, 1989.

Mickey Rourke, New York, 1994.

Stephen Sprouse, New York, 1992.

Fran Drescher, New York, 1994.

Tom Hanks, Los Angeles, 1997.

Kate Moss, John Galliano, Paris, 1993.

john galliano

Ask anyone who knows me and they will tell you that I am a huge fan of John Galliano. He inspires everyone who works with him to do their best, to push themselves further. And it all comes together beautifully. Every last detail is perfection. He understands visuals so well—whether it is a snapshot portrait of him or backstage at one of his shows—it is always a phenomenal photo. I remember one of the first shows of his I ever went to. Backstage was very crowded, full of the most beautiful girls in the business wearing enormous hoop skirts. John was taking the time to talk to each girl individually and fill their heads with stories and characters. Each girl got her own vision, her own story, individual attention, encouragement and praise directly from John. I overheard him telling Kate Moss: "It's *Gone With the Wind* and you're Scarlett O'Hara! Grab your skirt and run. Run, Kate, run! You're running against the wind—be careful the dress is heavy. Stop Kate! Now turn! Now run, Kate, Run!" The dress was so heavy she was practically falling over, yet somehow she remained stunning and graceful.

Ellen Von Unwerth, New York, 1992.

Blonde, New York, 1982.

Francesco Clemente, Paris, 1993.

William S. Burroughs, New York, 1992.

Todd Solondz, Los Angeles, 1999.

Philip Johnson, New York, 1994.

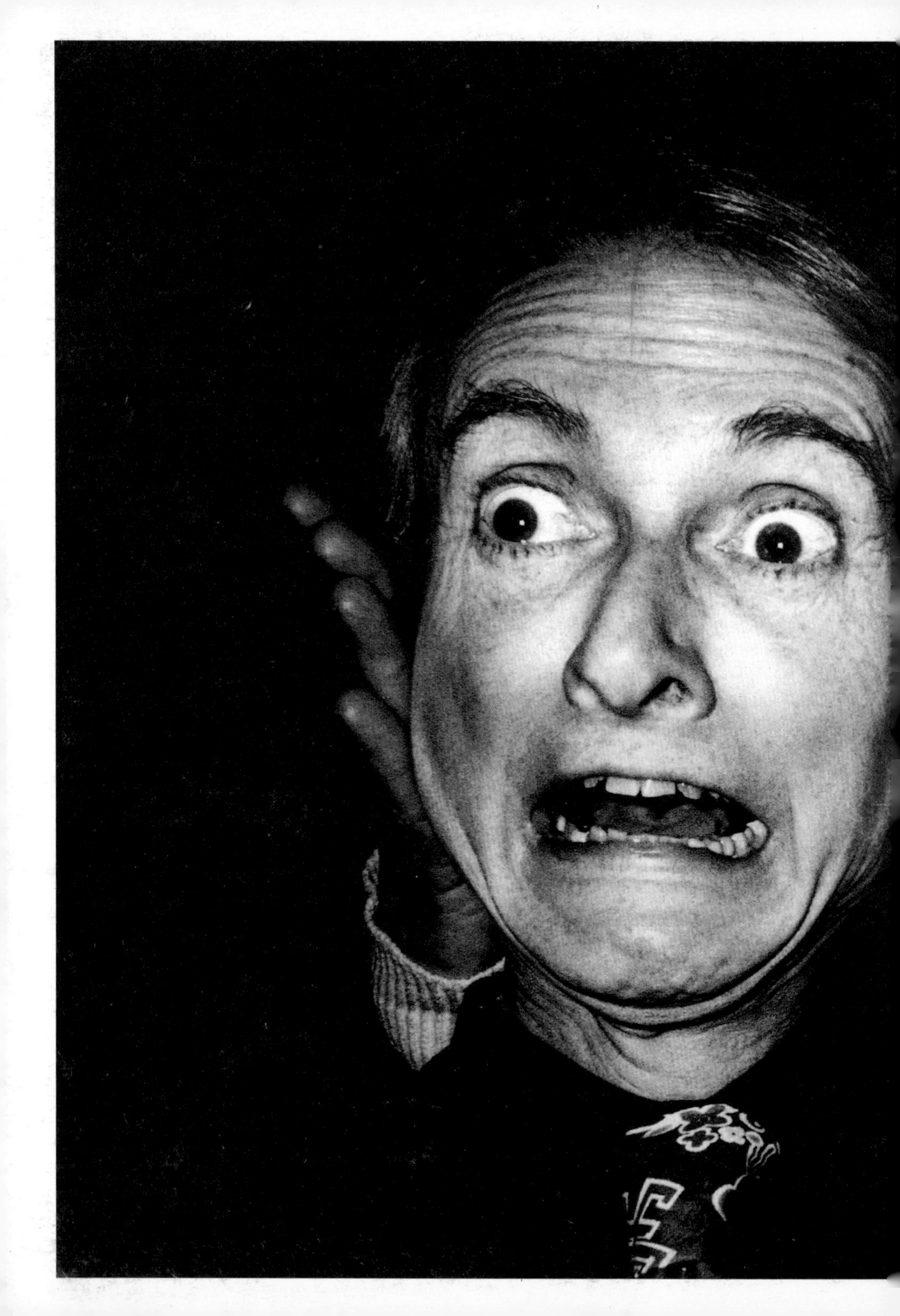

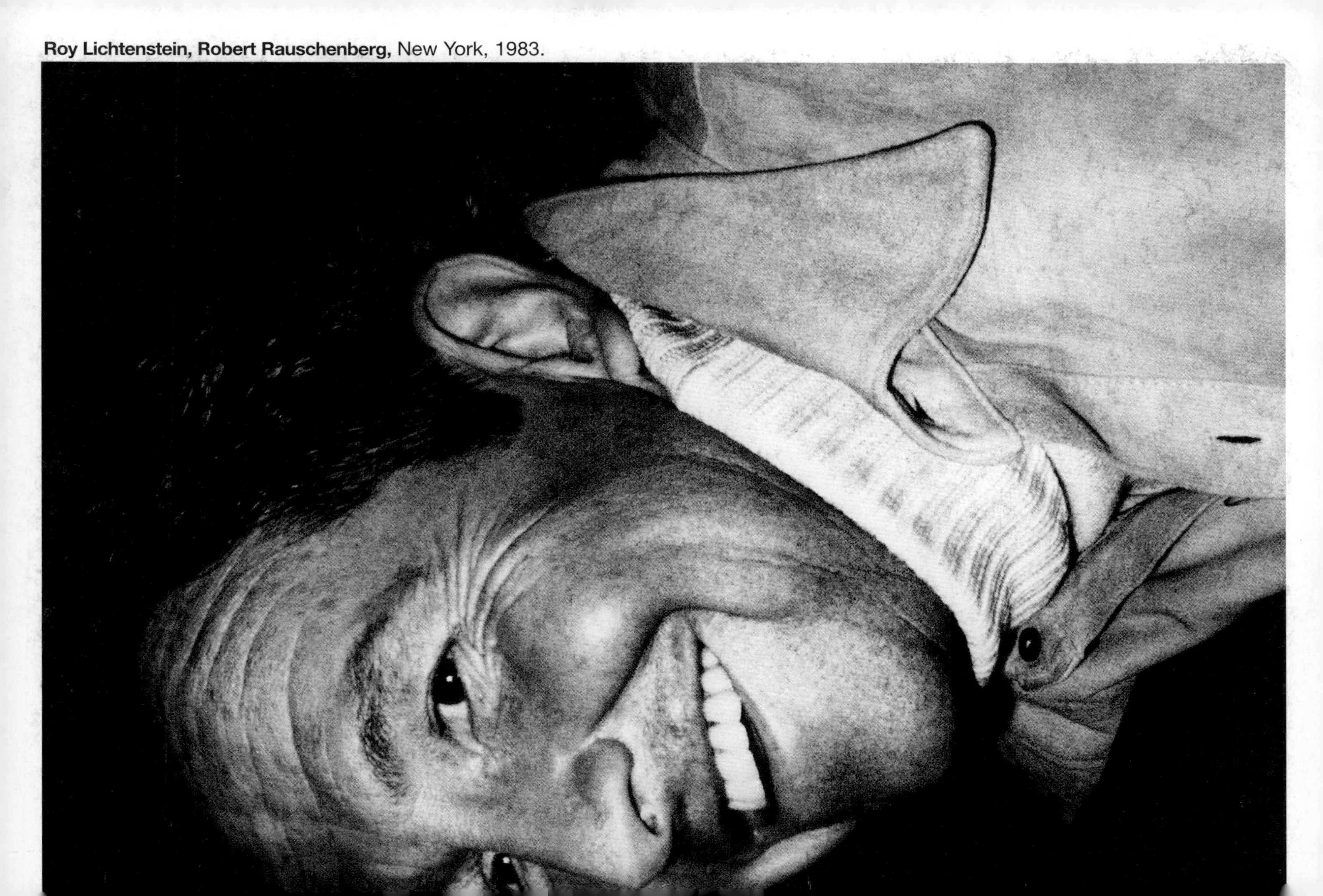

Roy Lichtenstein, Robert Rauschenberg, New York, 1983.

Toukie Smith, Pat Cleveland, Jerry Hall, New York, 1979.

Kate Moss, Milan, 1994.

Helmut Newton, Paris, 1996.

Hamilton South, Moana Pozzi, Milan, 1993.

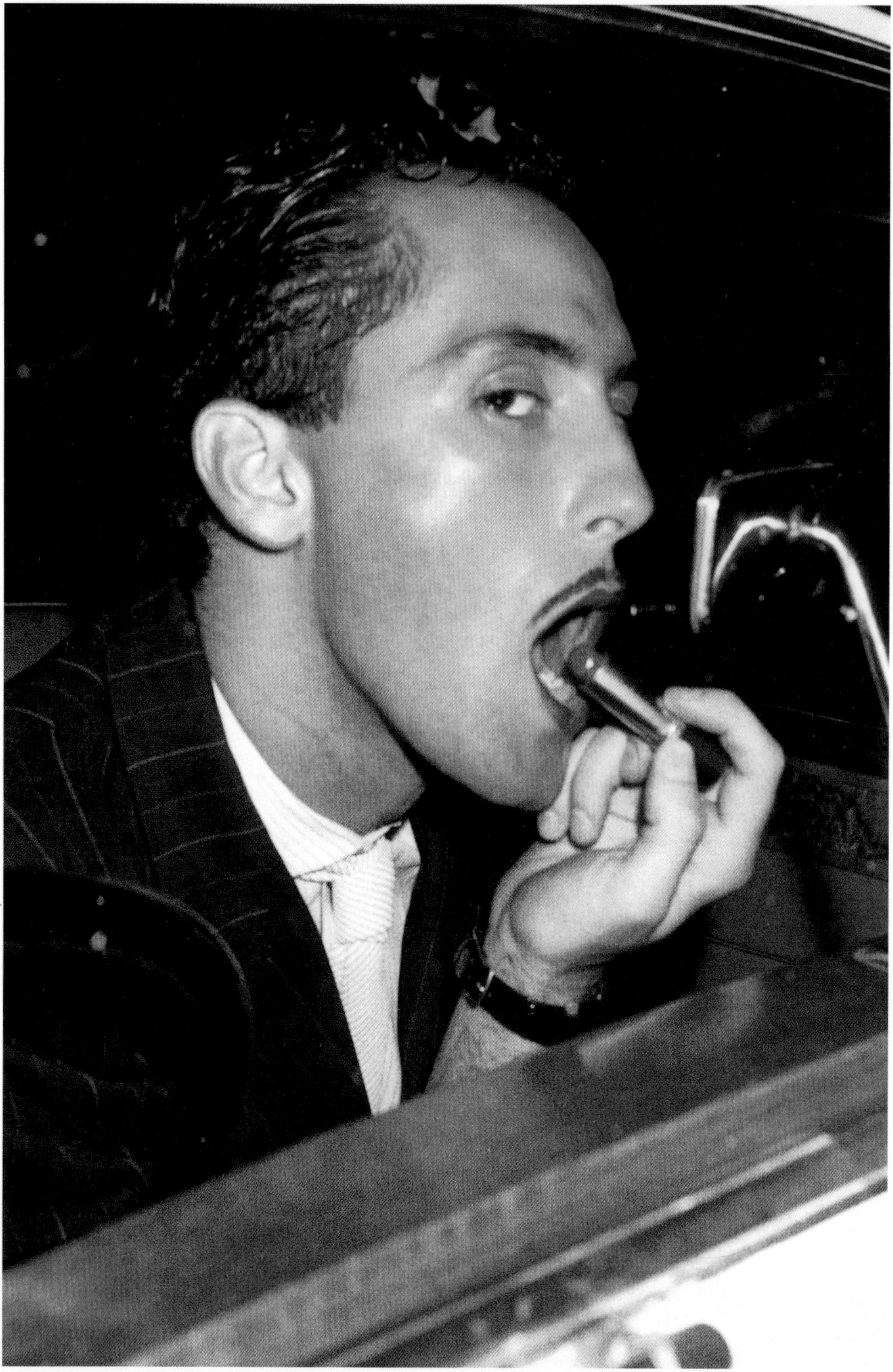

Latina Latuna, New York, 1978.

Fellini Circus, Paris, 1979.

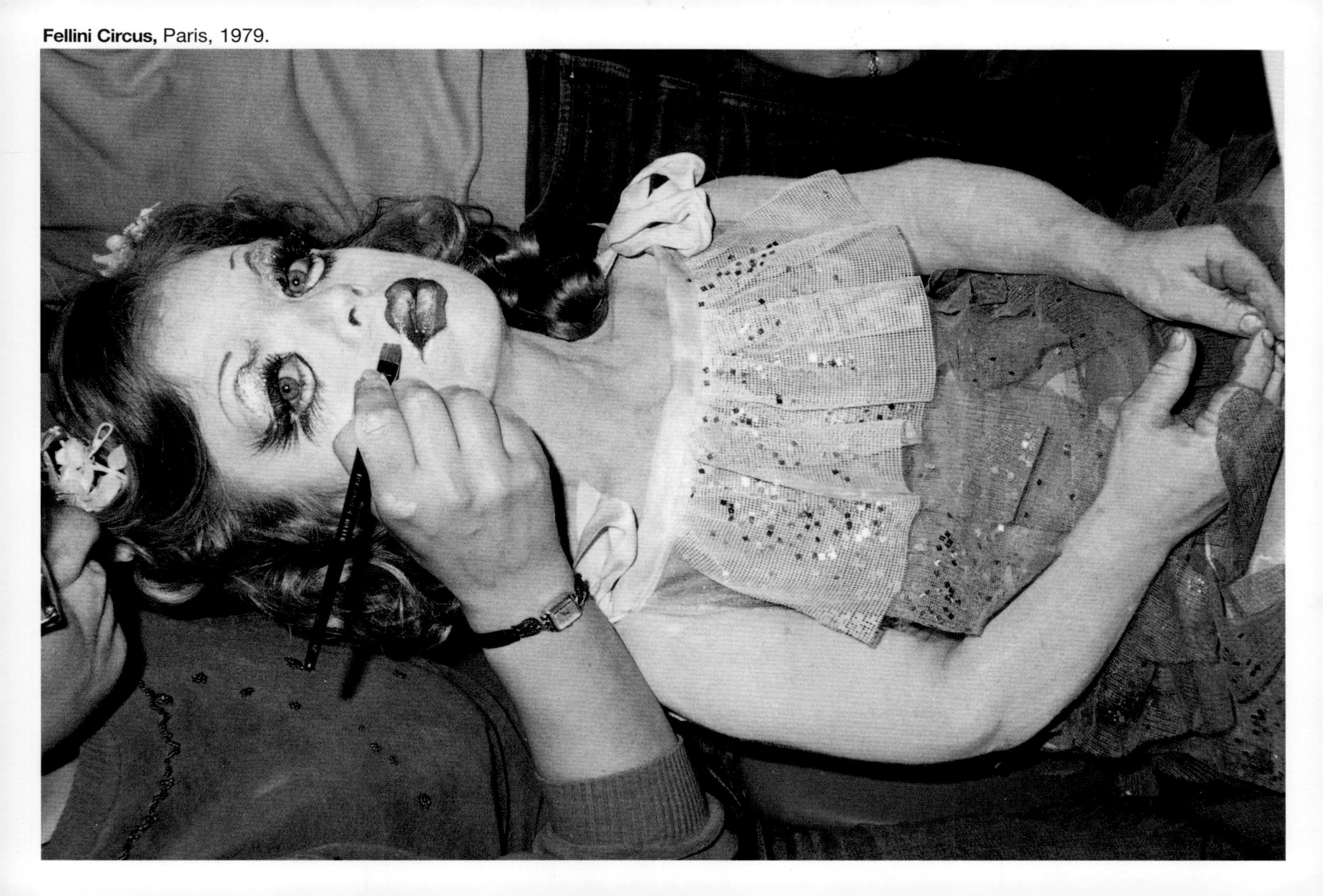

Drag queens, Fire Island, 1979.

Halston, Andy Warhol, New York, 1984.

andy warhol

Whenever, wherever I went out, Andy Warhol was there. He was always at the best parties—uptown, downtown, day or night. We had a lot in common: our love of nightlife and our love of people, but mostly we were both observers. We liked to watch situations unfold, absorb them, capture them forever and then share our visions with the world. On one of the many occasions on which I had the pleasure of Andy Warhol's company, he let me in on a little secret. He said, "You know Roxanne, I learned something from you." I was so curious to know what it was that I could teach Andy when he pulled out one camera from each pocket and said, "One for color and one for black and white."

Keith Haring, New York, 1985.

Divine, New York, 1979.

Clovis Ruffin and date, Paris, 1980.

Brenda Bergman, George Patterson, New York, 1977.

Terry and Bob Richardson, New York, 1996.

John Galliano, New York, 1996.

Kate Moss, Paris, 1993.

Pauline, Vincent Darre, Paris, 1981.

Humpty-Hump and Mystery the Cat, New York, 1990.

Earl Fatha Hines, New York, 1989.

Bootsy Collins, New York, 1994.

Johnny Depp, New York, 1994.

Vanessa Salle, Milan, 1994.

Isabella Rossellini, Milan, 1995.

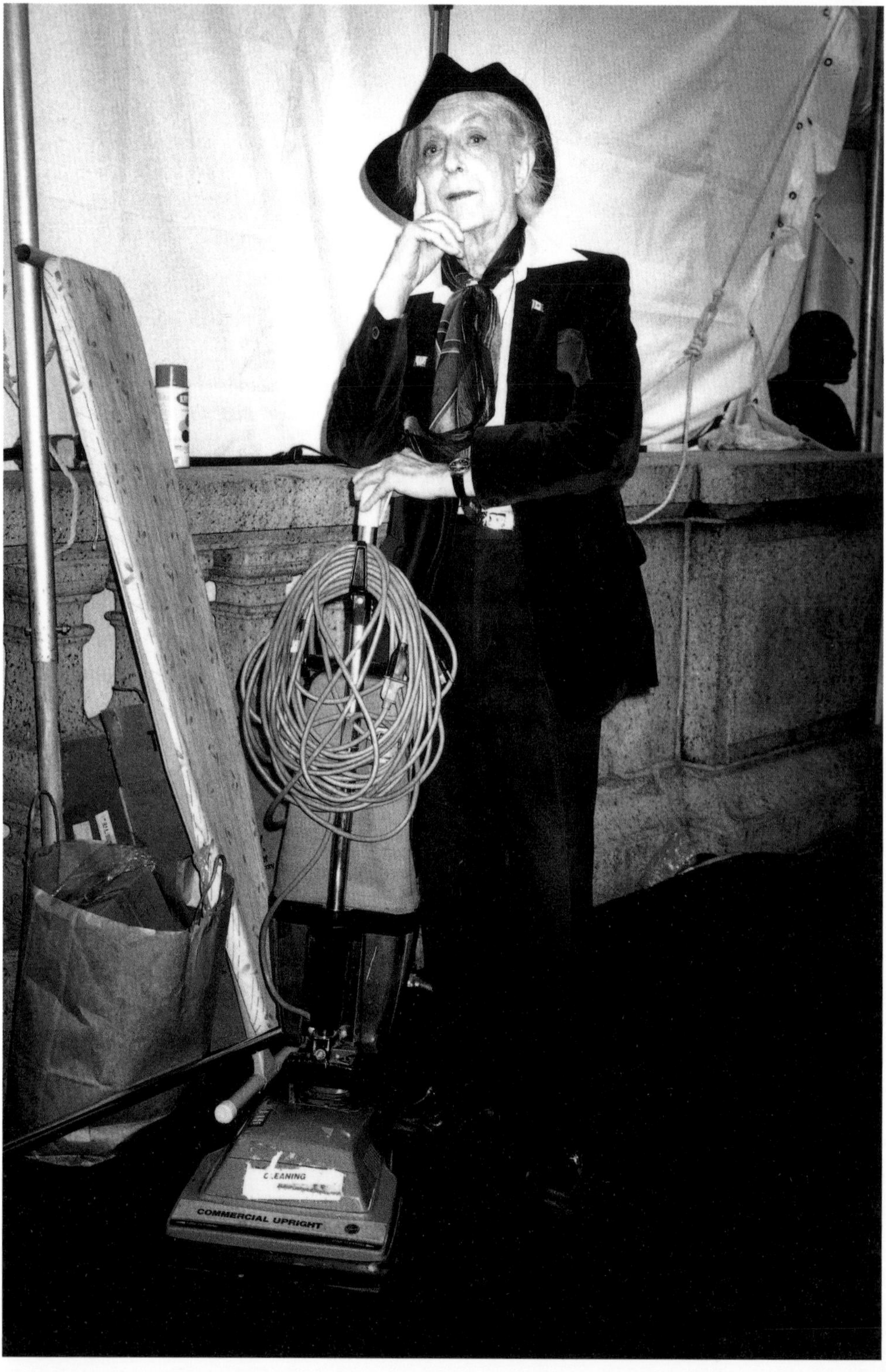

Quentin Crisp, New York, 1994.

quentin crisp was known for not cleaning. He didn't believe in it. He claimed that after four years, the dirt doesn't get any worse. Once I saw him backstage at a fashion show and there happened to be a vacuum cleaner there as well. "How funny," I thought and so I did a portrait of him and the vacuum cleaner.

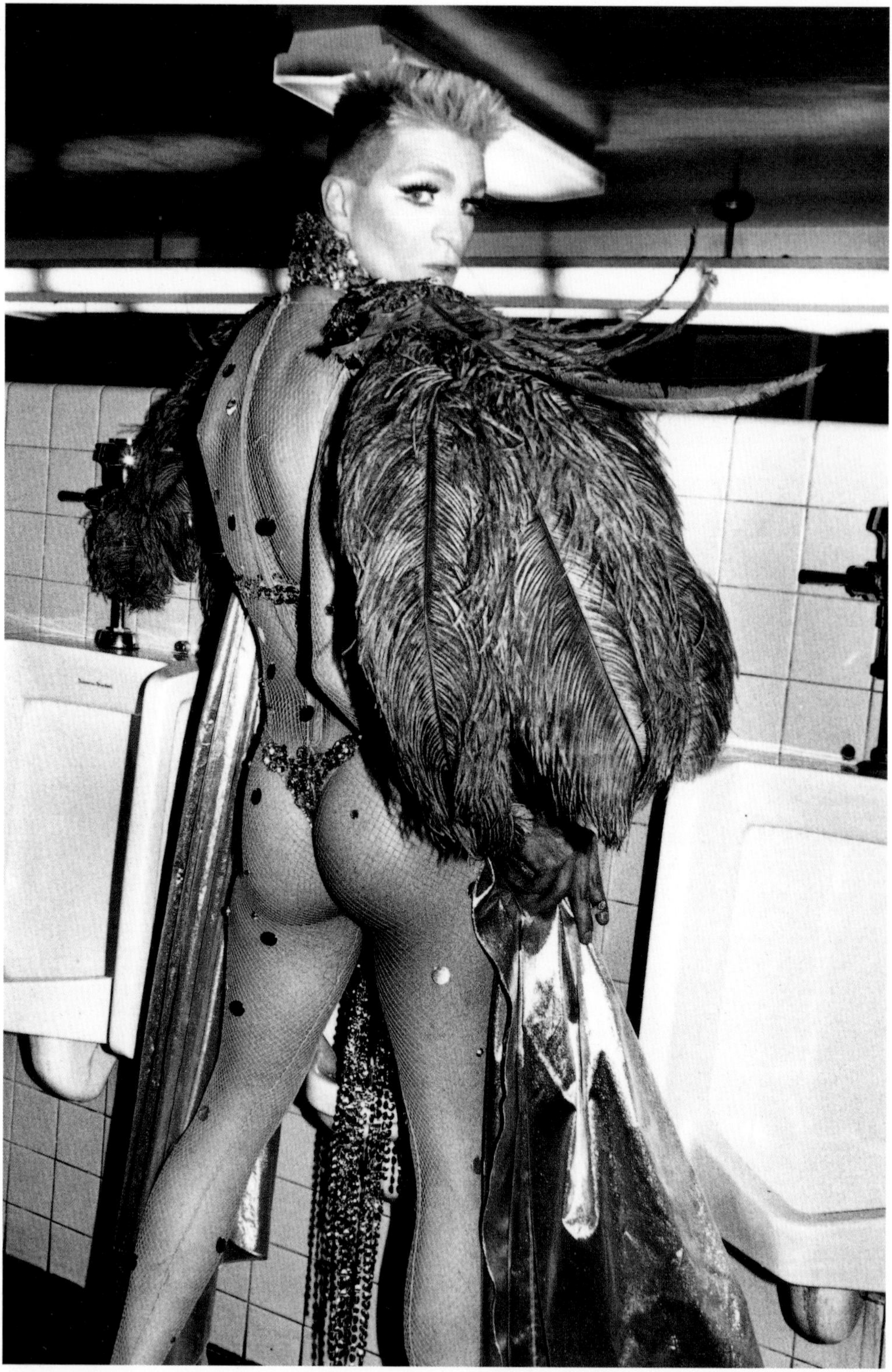

Love Ball, New York, 1989.

Sophie Dahl, Paris, 2000.

Dianne Brill, Paris, 1989.

Nude with beads, Paris, 1980.

Salvador Dalí, Janet Daly and a recipient of a kiss, New York, 1979.

salvador dalí

One year I was invited by a mutual acquaintance, Alana Garcia, to Salvador Dalí and Gala's New Year's Eve party. It was a fantastic party. I was so ecstatic to be there. Dalí was so easy to photograph because he couldn't resist playing to my camera. I foolishly left the party shortly after midnight. I will never forgive myself for leaving that party. It was the last time I ever saw him. It was a different age where celebrities were more approachable, more like everyone else. They enjoyed having their picture taken: it was an honor.

Lauren Hutton and chauffeur, New York, 1984.

Ralph Lauren, Diana Vreeland, New York, 1984.

Bill Blass, Diana Vreeland, New York, 1982.

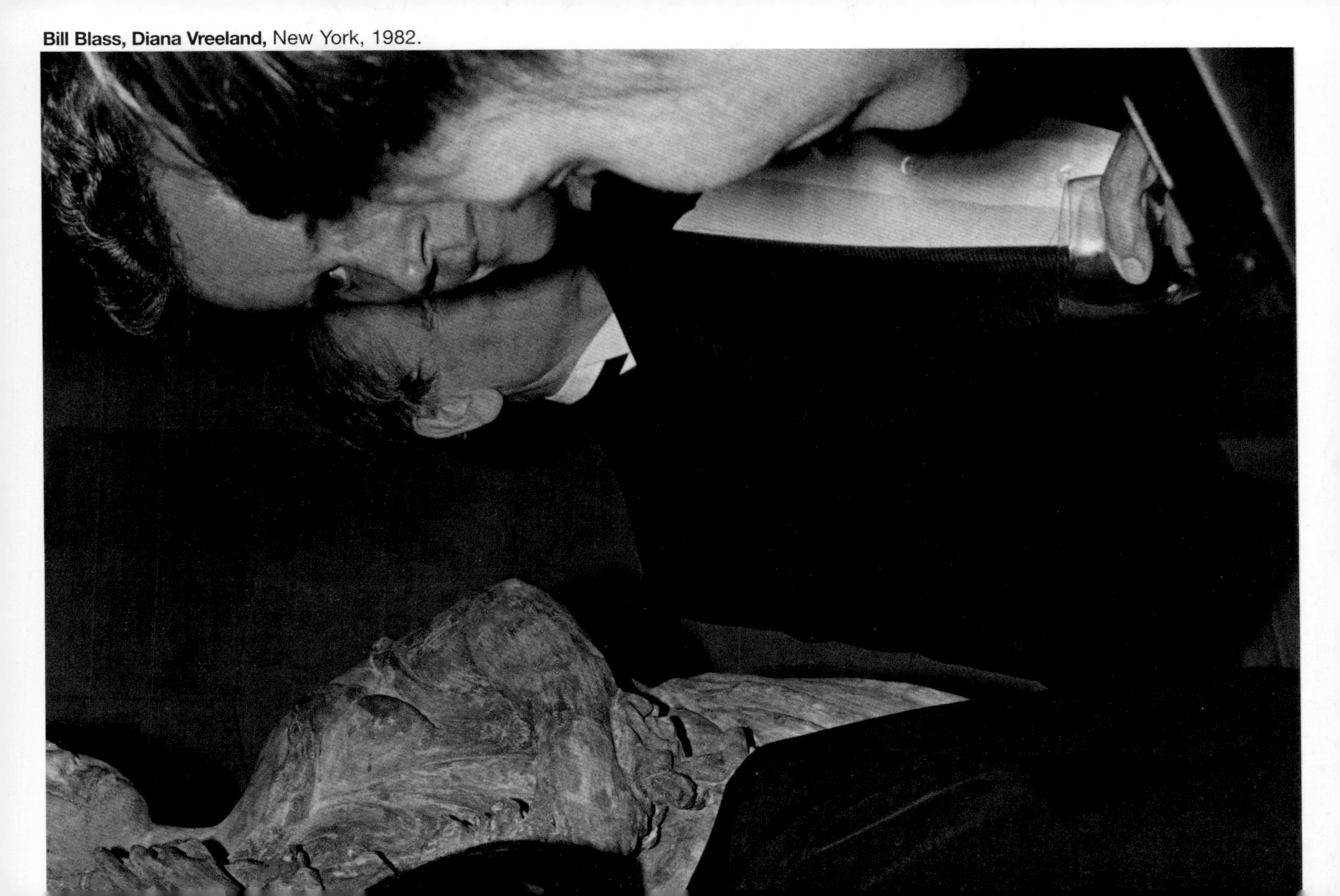

Michael Douglas, Sylvester Stallone, Cannes, 1993.

Jamie and Mike Cabreza, New York, 1999.

Fran Lebowitz, New York, 1984.

David Bowie, Nell Campbell, New York, 1991.

Sting, New York, 1985.

fran lebowitz

According to Fran Lebowitz I have more photographs of her than her mother does.

sting

The first time that I ever met Sting was at the Mudd Club. I introduced myself to him: “Hi, my name is Roxanne.” I told him how he had changed my life by writing the song “Roxanne.” Before that song, no one could get my name right: Rosanna, Rosanne... He was gracious, friendly and quite charming. I remember how he held my hand and stared into my eyes while we spoke. Then, suddenly, he dropped my hand and looked away, muttering something about how his wife was looking at him. Many years later, I saw Sting at a Versace show with his true love Trudie. There was a swarm of photographers surrounding him, yelling out for him to “Do something different!” Sting replied, “Why don't you do something different?” And so I took a step forward and planted a big hug and a kiss on his lips. Trudie walked over and he introduced us, “This is Roxanne, I wrote the song for her.”

The Misfits, New York, 1979.

Hell's Angels, New York, 1983.

Hell's Angels, New York, 1983.

Joey Ramone, New York, 1978.

Susanne Bartsch's party, New York, 1994.

BANKY

Ron Wood, Jo Howard, New York, 1988.

Gloria Gaynor, New York, 1979.

John Lee Hooker, New York, 1990.

Wesley Snipes, Eartha Kitt, New York, 1996.

Calypso singer, New York, 1981.

Joan Collins, Michael Hutchence, Valentino, Paris, 1992.

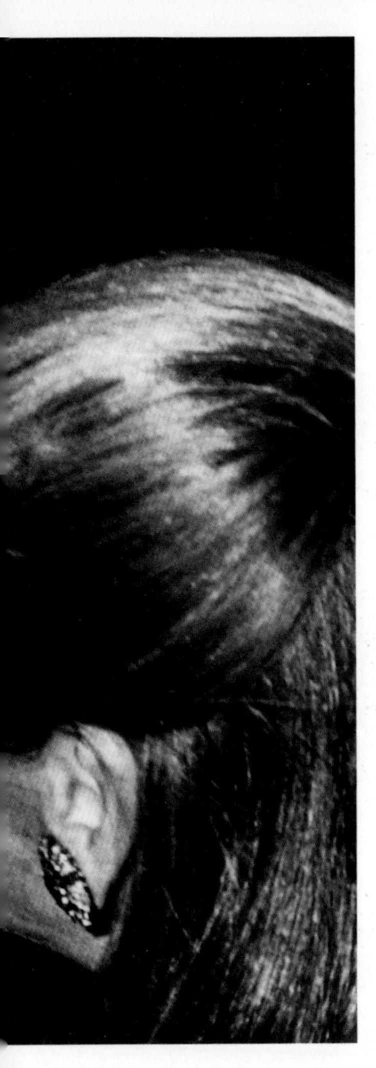

joan collins

Like many designers, Valentino throws great star-studded parties. At one in particular, Michael Hutchence and Joan Collins were both there. Michael, though surrounded by many beautiful women, his girlfriend Helena Christensen, and even some fans, was dying to meet Joan Collins and asked me if I could introduce him. Her elegance and sophistication really appealed to him. He found it extremely sexy. I think he was trying to seduce her, but all the while, she had him eating out of her hand.

Leonardo DiCaprio, Paris, 1995.

Kate Moss, Paris, 1995.

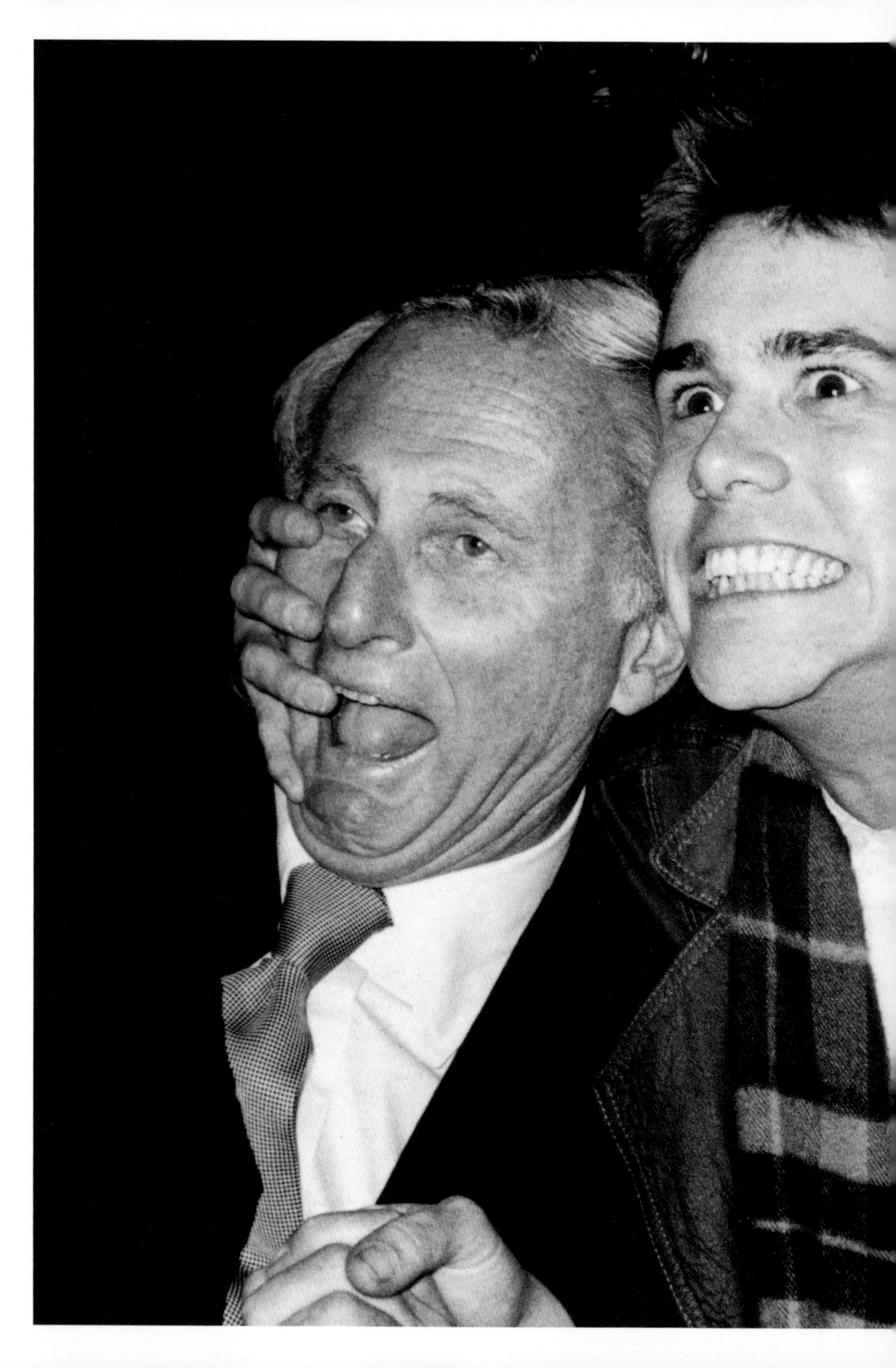

Jim Carrey, Lauren Hutton and friend, New York, 1985.

Annabelle Nielson Rothschild, John Galliano, Monte Carlo, 2000.

annabelle nielson

Helmut Newton had a big party in Monte Carlo and people from all the walks of life traveled from around the world to be there. The party was held outdoors and it was a beautiful night. I was so thrilled to be there covering it for Italian *Vogue*. I was snapping shots of this person and that person, when suddenly there was a big commotion at the entrance. Cameras were flashing so brightly and endlessly, photographers yelling out to make sure they got the photo. I was terribly curious. Then I saw John Galliano and his entourage turn the corner. Annabelle Nielson Rothschild was among his usual crowd, wearing a stunning dress that John made specifically for her to wear to Helmut Newton's party that night. It was no wonder the photographers were going mad outside. She was wearing a sheer black spiderweb dress. Everything her little G-string did not cover could be seen. Later that evening, the dress became even racier when Annabelle went swimming in the middle of the party with John and his crew. Annabelle's spiderweb dress clung to her wet skin and she stole the show that evening.

Club couple kissing, New York, 1989.

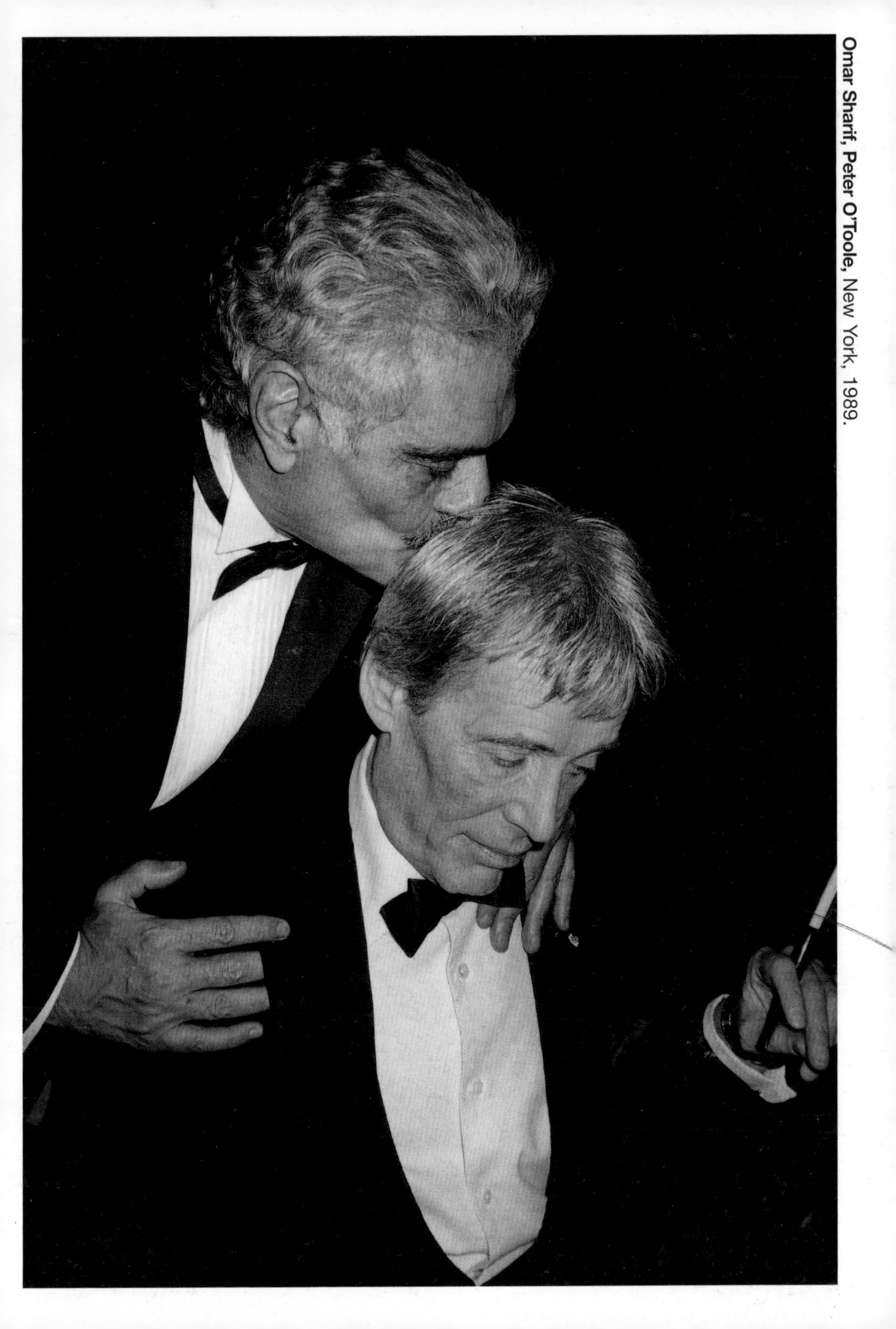

Omar Sharif, Peter O'Toole, New York, 1989.

Guy Cuevas, Paris, 1981.

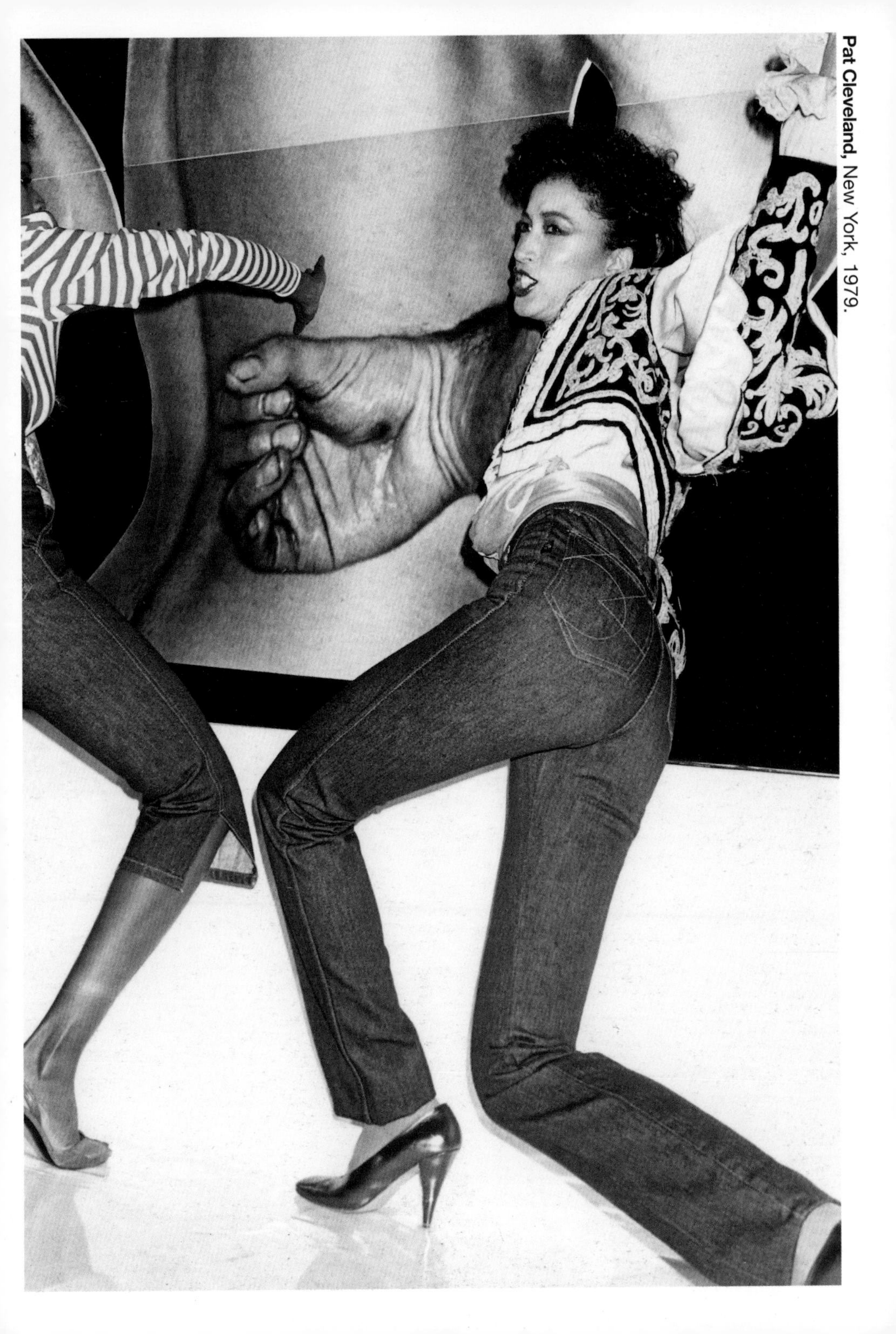

Pat Cleveland, New York, 1979.

Baroness, The Empress, Atlantic City, 1995.

Richard Avedon, Irving Penn, Helmut Newton, New York, 1983.

richard avedon irving penn helmut newton

I went to Alexander Liberman's opening at the Gagosian Gallery. I got there early because I was covering the event for Condé Nast and didn't want to miss a thing. I was also looking forward to seeing his show. I was taking a photo of Liberman, when suddenly I looked up and there was Helmut Newton. When I looked up again, I saw that Richard Avedon had arrived. I was thrilled and so excited to take their picture and just as I got the three of them together, I looked up a third time. My heart skipped a beat as I saw Irving Penn "the great" walk through the door. Hardly anyone else knew who he was. It was not difficult for Liberman, or anyone else for that matter, to read the excitement written all over my face. I couldn't help myself, I had to ask Mr. Penn, who hates having his picture taken, to join the trio and make it a quartet. I quickly snapped off a few shots and then Liberman slipped out and said: "Why not get a shot of the three greats together." Needless to say, I seized the moment and shot off as many as my camera would allow. I feel so blessed and honored to have been there to capture that moment on film forever.

Helena Christensen, Karl Lagerfeld, Anna Wintour, Milan, 1994.

Emmanuel Ungaro and model, Paris, 1991.

André Leon Talley, Polly Mellen, Carlyne Cerf, Paris, 1994.

Domenico Dolce, Azzedine Alaïa, Rifat Ozbek, Stefano Gabbana, Milan, 1994.

Tom Ford, Orlando Pita, Kate Moss, Milan, 2000.

kate moss

There aren't too many models, or women for that matter, like Kate Moss. She never refuses me a minute of her time to take a picture. Whether she is posing or laughing candidly, or even unaware of my camera, she somehow gives it her all time and again. It is always a great photo. Kate is a stunning beauty, who can also easily play the girl next door. She is fun, full of life, sweet, friendly, professional and real, a real star without ever being a diva. As far as I'm concerned, there is no such thing as a bad picture of Kate Moss. At a recent Gucci show, I was thrilled to see Kate was back at work. It was the Spring collection and the girls were wearing little t-shirts and bikini bottoms and were being sprayed with water before they went out on the runway. Someone was slowly spraying Kate when Tom Ford said "Give me that!" He took the bottle and started spraying Kate. He had a mischevious look on his face. I could tell that he was really enjoying this part of his job. She leaned forward a bit to make sure that he was getting her everywhere. I knew it would be a great photo. It is. Even soaked with freezing water, Kate is beautiful.

Gisele Bundchen, New York, 2000.

Linda Evangelista, New York, 1990.

Vivitar
2800

Peter Lindbergh, Arthur Elgort, Patrick Demarchelier, New York, 1989.

Bryony Miss Agent Provocateur, Paris, 1995.

Yohji Yamamoto, Paris, 1992.

Calvin Klein, New York, 1979.

Kate Moss, Paris, 1994.

June Newton, Andrée Putman, Paris, 1981.

Gina Lollobrigida, Linda Evangelista, Rome, 1991.

linda evangelista gina lollobrigida

The night of Valentino's 30th anniversary in Rome, the weather was wet and dreary. But that didn't put a damper on the party or its guests. Everyone was dressed in their most elegant attire: gowns, furs, and jewels. Everyone who was anyone made their way through the monsoon in order to show their respects. It didn't matter that everything, including the dance floor, was soaking wet. Linda Evangelista was there, looking stunning and timeless, and I asked her to sit beside Gina Lollobrigida for a photograph. They were both in pink gowns and it reminded me of the old Hollywood photographs of the 1950s.

Gisele Bundchen, Milan, 1999.

Celia Cruz, New York, 1999.

Campagnolo

Patrick Kelly, Iman, Grace Jones, Naomi Campbell, Paris, 1989.

“Frankenfurther” impersonator, Rocky Horror Show, New York, 1979.

Brooke Astor, New York, 1989.

Miles Davis, New York, 1986.

Michele Rimbault, Paris, 1989.

The Nicholas Brothers, New York, 1989.

Pat Cleveland, New York, 1980.

Sean “Puffy” Combs, New York, 2000.

Wu Tang Clan, New York, 1999.

Simon Doonan, Paris, 1993.

simon doonan

I was shooting a big story for *L'Uomo Vogue* with Paul Sinclaire in Milan. We were shooting at the restaurant Di Giacomo, which is famous for its meat dishes. I wanted Joel West to be eating the meat off of a bone. The restaurant claimed they didn't have any bones even though they served so much meat. We insisted they must have bones and they said the only bones they had were in the garbage. So I made them go into the garbage to find us a good bone, wash it off carefully and cook it up. They did such a good job of it I had to keep reminding Joel that the bone came out of the garbage. The photo I have of Simon Doonan (*Confessions of a Window Dresser*) eating some sort of bird was the inspiration for the Joel West photo. But the funny thing here is that Simon is also just pretending. Simon is actually a vegetarian. He was responding to Gene Pressman, of Barney's, who said that he was going to teach Simon how to be a real man—by eating meat and smoking cigars.

Azzedine Alaïa, Tina Turner, New York, 1986.

Ru Paul, Dr. Ruth, New York, 1994.

David Bowie, Chandra North, New York, 1995.

Matt Dillon, Fabiola Deracasa, New York, 1999.

Spice Girls, New York, 1997.

Bianca Jagger, New York, 1988.

Tina Turner, New York, 1979.

Willem Dafoe, Cannes, 1993.

Philip Glass, New York, 1987.

Lolo Ferrari, Jacques Moisant, Paris, 1997.

Ivana and Donald Trump, New York, 1988.

Dolly Parton, New York, 1984.

dolly parton

I was shooting Dolly Parton for *Interview* magazine. I had to be there at 9 a.m. I was told that I had a half hour to set up and another half hour to shoot her, but by time the reporter was done with the interview, I only had ten minutes to shoot, and that made me a little nervous. I was really looking forward to meeting and photographing Dolly and getting another great photo of her for my archives. I had only photographed her in passing, at crowded gala events and parties. This was my chance at something more personal and intimate. She walked into the room with her tiny frame and her larger-than-life presence, and that made me more at ease. I began to enjoy my brief time with such an amazing woman. Dolly is gracious, open, warm, charming, genuine, delightful. Now I know what they mean by "southern hospitality." The ten minutes and three rolls flew by. I don't think many people realize how tiny she is. She is a master of illusion in that regard. She was wearing these super-high heels, with platforms and spikes at the end of her slender legs and delicate feet. She has remarkable legs and I couldn't help commenting on them: "You have the legs of a drag queen," I boldly said to her, hoping she realized that I meant it as a compliment. She obviously did because she said to me in a southern drawl: "Why Honey, I always said that if I had been born a man that I would have been a drag queen."

Matt Damon, Ben Affleck, Los Angeles, 1999.

Ashley Judd, New York, 1995.

Emma Balfour, Paris, 1995.

Milla Jovovich, Paris, 2000.

John Galliano show, Paris, 1993.

Cyndi Lauper, New York, 1997.

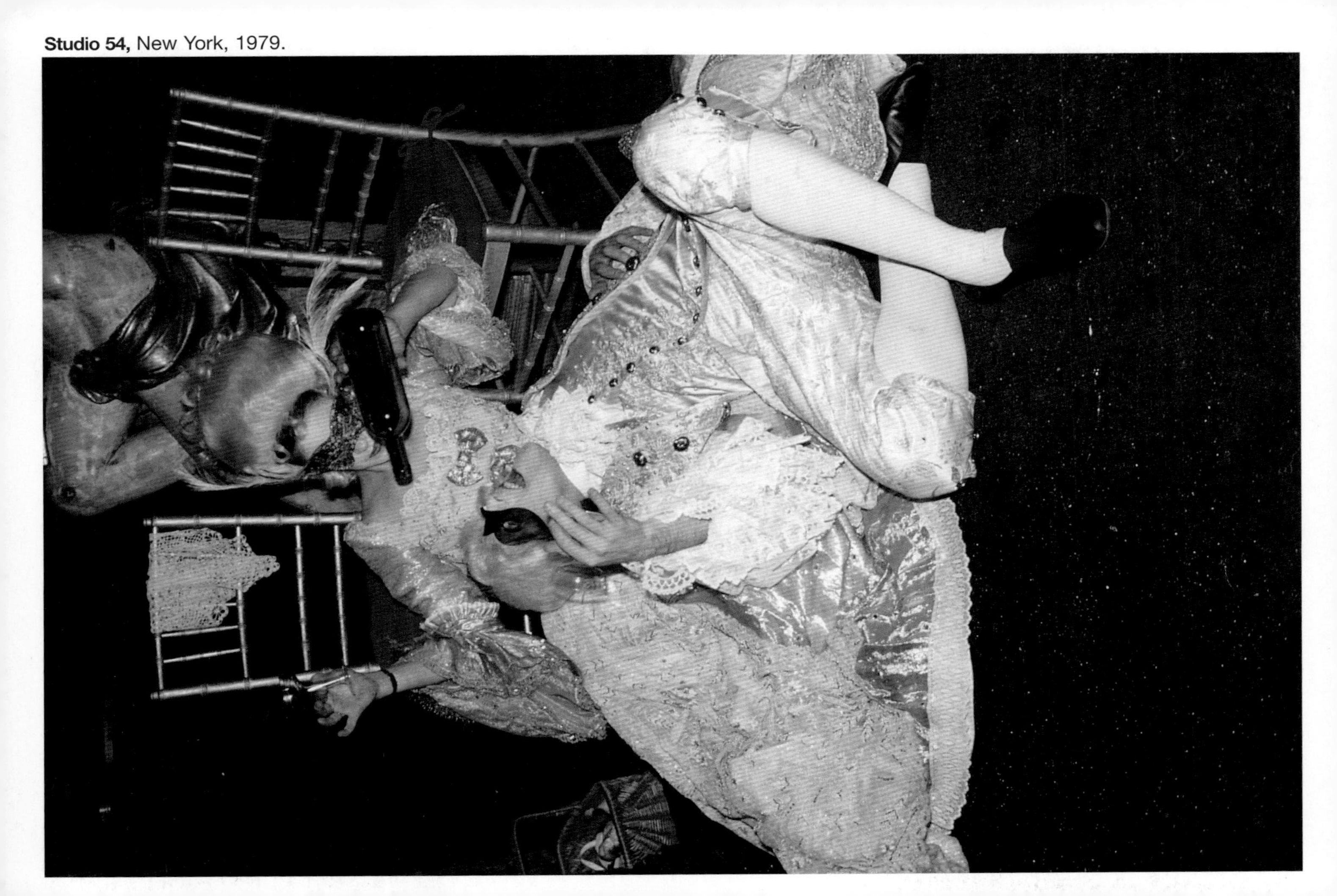

Studio 54, New York, 1979.

Gwyneth Paltrow, Los Angeles, 2000.

Anna Piaggi, Paris, 1986.

Suzanne Aichinger, Paris, 1998.

Yves Saint Laurent and models, Paris, 1985.

yves saint laurent

The first time I was in Paris covering the shows, I was extremely lucky to meet Yves Saint Laurent and Andy Warhol on the top of the Eiffel Tower. It was a moment I will never forget. It was so fabulous and glamorous, the kind of stuff that dreams are made of. And yet it seemed so natural. It somehow made sense that I was there at that moment. I felt as if I belonged there. I took it as a good omen that I was doing the right thing, that I was where I should be, on the right track, and off to an amazing start. This was my life. Many years later, backstage at a Saint Laurent show, I asked Yves if he remembered the first time we met. He smiled at me and said, "Of course I do, we met for the first time on the top of the Eiffel Tower."

The McGuire Sisters, New York, 1995.

Drag queens, New York, 1982.

Claude Montana, Wallis Franken, Yves Saint Laurent, Paris, 1993.

wallis franken

After many years of being Claude Montana's muse, Wallis Franken was finally going to be his wife. A longtime friend of Wallis' and her family, I was very excited for her; she was so delighted to be getting married. On the way to the ceremony, we got stuck in ridiculous amounts of traffic. We saw an old burgundy Cadillac on the side of the road. Cadillacs are not a common sight in Paris, so we sat up and took notice. The chauffeur was leaning on the door and as we drove past, we saw someone in white sitting in the back, applying blush. We finally arrived at the courthouse, and, thankfully, we hadn't missed the ceremony. Soon after we arrived, we saw the same burgundy Cadillac pull into the courtyard. The chauffeur parked the car and went around to the passenger-side door and helped a radiant Wallis out of the front seat, and then Claude from the back. We had quite a giggle realizing that it wasn't the bride who was blushing this time, but the groom.

Christy Turlington, Kate Moss, Los Angeles, 1994.

Tina Chow, Fran Lebowitz, New York, 1980.

Nan Kempner, Fran Stark, Jacqueline de Ribes, New York, 1984.

Friend, Bill Blass, Nan Kempner, Jerry Zipkin, New York, 1989.

Carmen, Horst P. Horst, New York, 1994.

Virginia Melhado, Freddy Melhado, Carroll Petrie, Milton Petrie, New York, 1982.

Robert De Niro, Al Pacino, New York, 1982.

Baron Rothschild and friend, Paris, 1989.

Sophia Loren, Paris, 1994.

sophia loren is an icon of classic beauty. I recall once, during the years of Gianfranco Ferré, she was at a Dior party. She was sitting all alone at a large table. There were many other younger actresses at the party as well. As people started to sit down, and the tables began to fill up, I remarked that the seats closest to Sophia Loren were still empty. None of the other actresses would sit next to her because she was so radiant and beautiful they were afraid their looks would pale next to her. A few of them even took their name tags and moved them to another table.

176

Elizabeth Taylor, New York, 1982.

Audrey Hepburn, Diana Vreeland, Robert Wolders, New York, 1983.

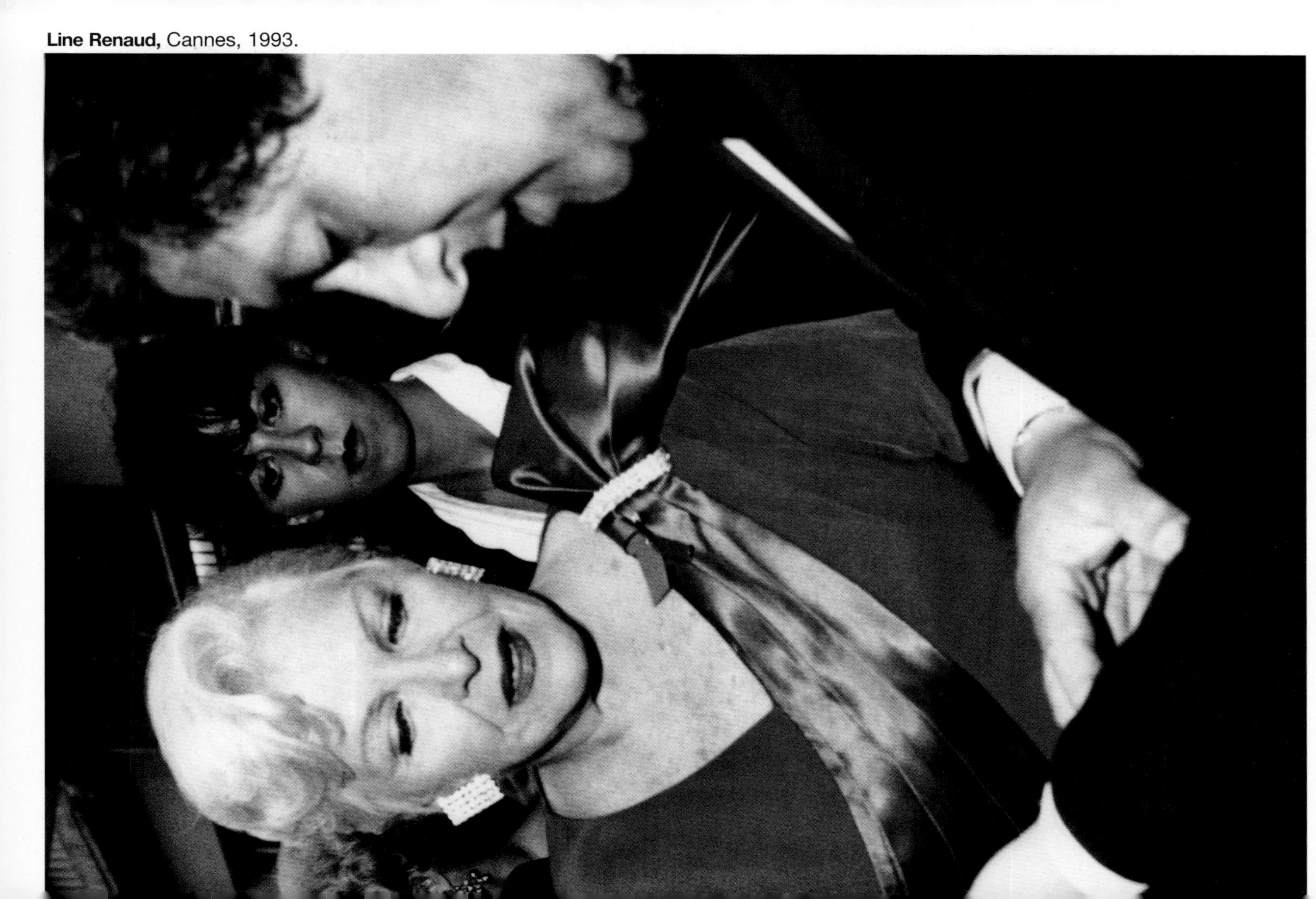

Line Renaud, Cannes, 1993.

Christian Lacroix, Karl Lagerfeld, Anna Wintour, Gianni Versace, New York, 1992.

Karl Lagerfeld, New York, 1991.

Jean-Paul Gaultier, Madonna, Paris, 1990.

Vivienne Westwood show, Paris, 1995.

Isaac Mizrahi masks, New York, 1996.

Brooklyn Academy of Music, New York, 1989.

laurie anderson

At one of Laurie Anderson's performances at the Brooklyn Academy of Music, masks were handed out to everyone. She asked the audience to put them on and then went over to an old-fashioned camera and began taking pictures of the audience. I looked around and thought that it was such a great image, I had to have one for myself. Not wanting to ruin her photo, I kept jumping up to take the photo and then would quickly sit back down. Later she asked me what I was doing jumping up and down throughout her performance. I told her that I didn't want to ruin her photo. She laughed and said, "There was no film in that camera, I am a performance artist."

Mollie Moon, New York, 1989.

Carolyn Murphy, Paris, 1996.

Shalom Harlow and pet, Paris, 1994.

Lillian Montevecchi, New York, 1982.

Wallis Franken, Kristen McMenamy, Larissa, New York, 1992.

Theo Kogan, New York, 1997.

Le Palace, Paris, 1980.

Eartha Kitt, New York, 1994.

Ellen Von Unwerth, Mario Testino, New York, 1993.

Herb Ritts, Christy Turlington, Steven Meisel, New York, 1989.

Polly Mellen, New York, 1991.

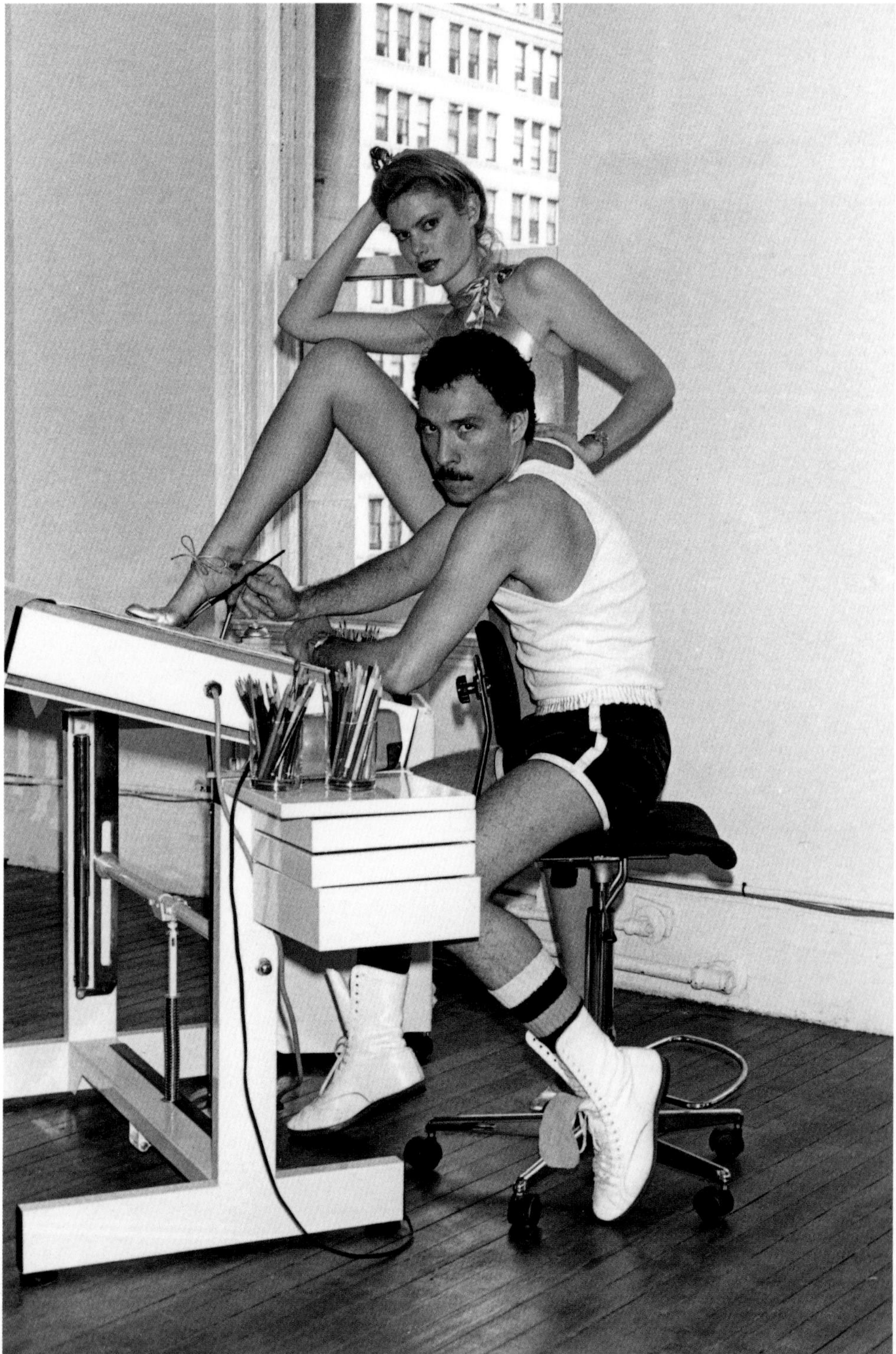

Antonio Lopez, Jane Thorvaldson, New York, 1977.

antonio lopez

I first met Antonio Lopez while studying at the Fashion Institute of Technology. My earliest memory of him is him salsa dancing in the cafeteria. I would see a lot more of both him and his dancing. He was extremely handsome, and a great dancer (he helped to refine my own salsa moves), but above all he was an amazing illustrator. He drew on everything! Every scrap of paper, napkins, table-cloths... He was talented, driven, charming, sexy, charismatic, funny, kind. Everyone wanted to be close to him: men, women, even children. He knew who would get along and would introduce them to each other. He had an amazing understanding of fashion, people and life. He also had an amazing eye and used it for many things, one of which was discovering some of the top models of the time: Donna Jordan, Toukie Smith, Pat Cleveland, Grace Jones, Jessica Lange and Jerry Hall. His illustrations and influences changed the way people viewed fashion.

Antonio Lopez and friends, New York, 1982.

Andy Warhol, New York, 1985.

Fire Island, 1979.

John Granito, Antonio Lopez, Fire Island, 1979.

Short shorts, Fire Island, 1978.

Sarah Kapp, Antonio Lopez, New York, 1980.

The Village People, New York, 1980.

Neon Woman, New York, 1977.

Terry Richardson, Katie Barker, Paris, 1999.

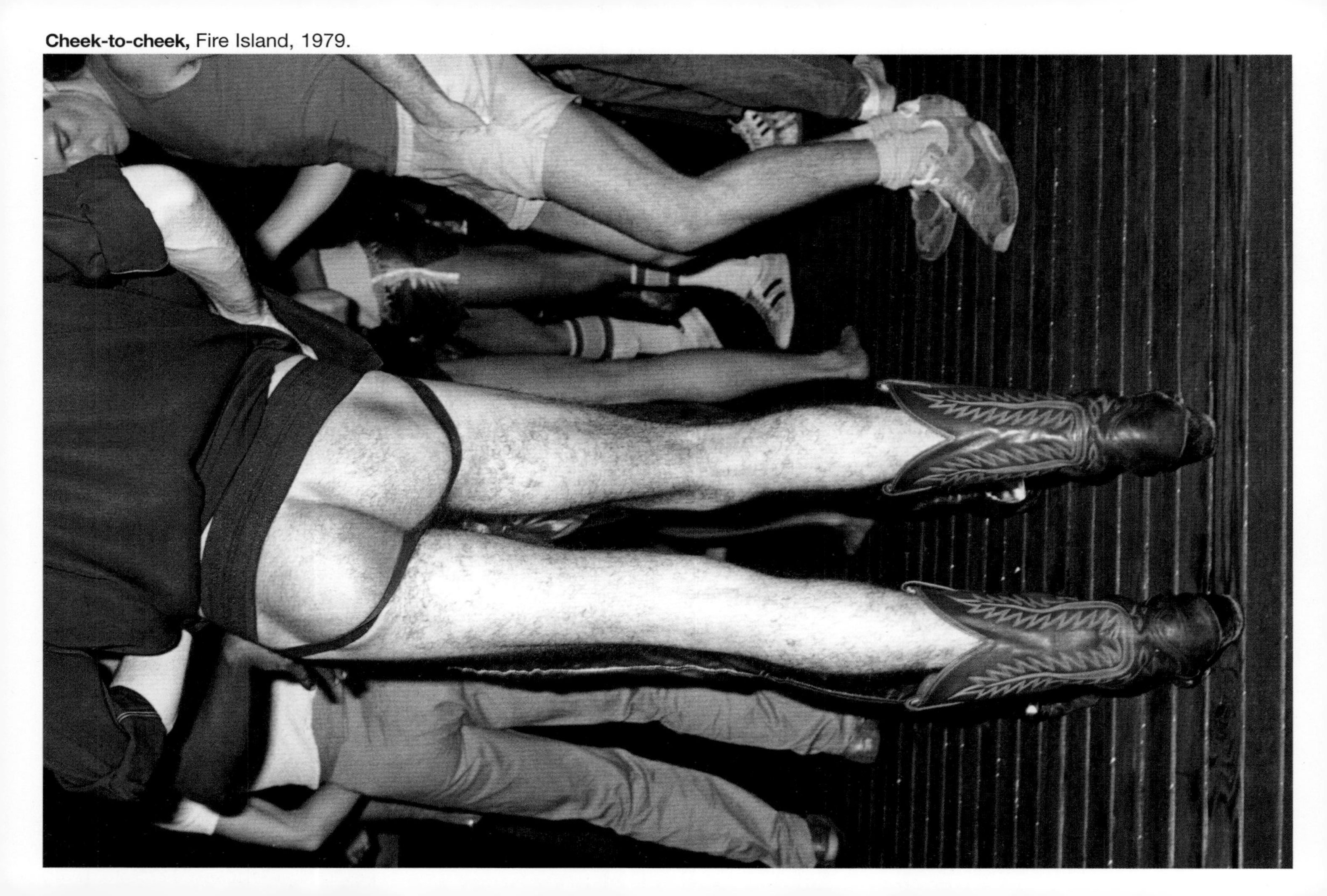

Cheek-to-cheek, Fire Island, 1979.

Aliens on Broadway, New York, 1995.

aliens I NEVER leave a camera empty. I always load the camera with whatever film I have on hand. Color or black and white, it doesn't matter as long as I don't miss the moment. I was at the *Paper* luncheon at Indochine. The luncheon was finished and so was my roll of film. I saw no reason to put in a new roll because I was on my way home. When I turned onto Broadway, there were six aliens walking up the street straight toward me. I couldn't believe my eyes or my luck. "Wait!" I screamed as I threw my bag down on the sidewalk and started searching for a roll of film. At last I found one and loaded my camera and snapped the moment up. I have no idea where they came from or what they were doing there. It wasn't even close to Halloween. It was quite bizarre, but wonderful too.

Lavinia Co-Op, Susanne Bartsch's party, New York, 1997.

Klaus Nomi, New York, 1979.

Partygoers, New York, 1980.

Amanda Lepore, New York, 1999.

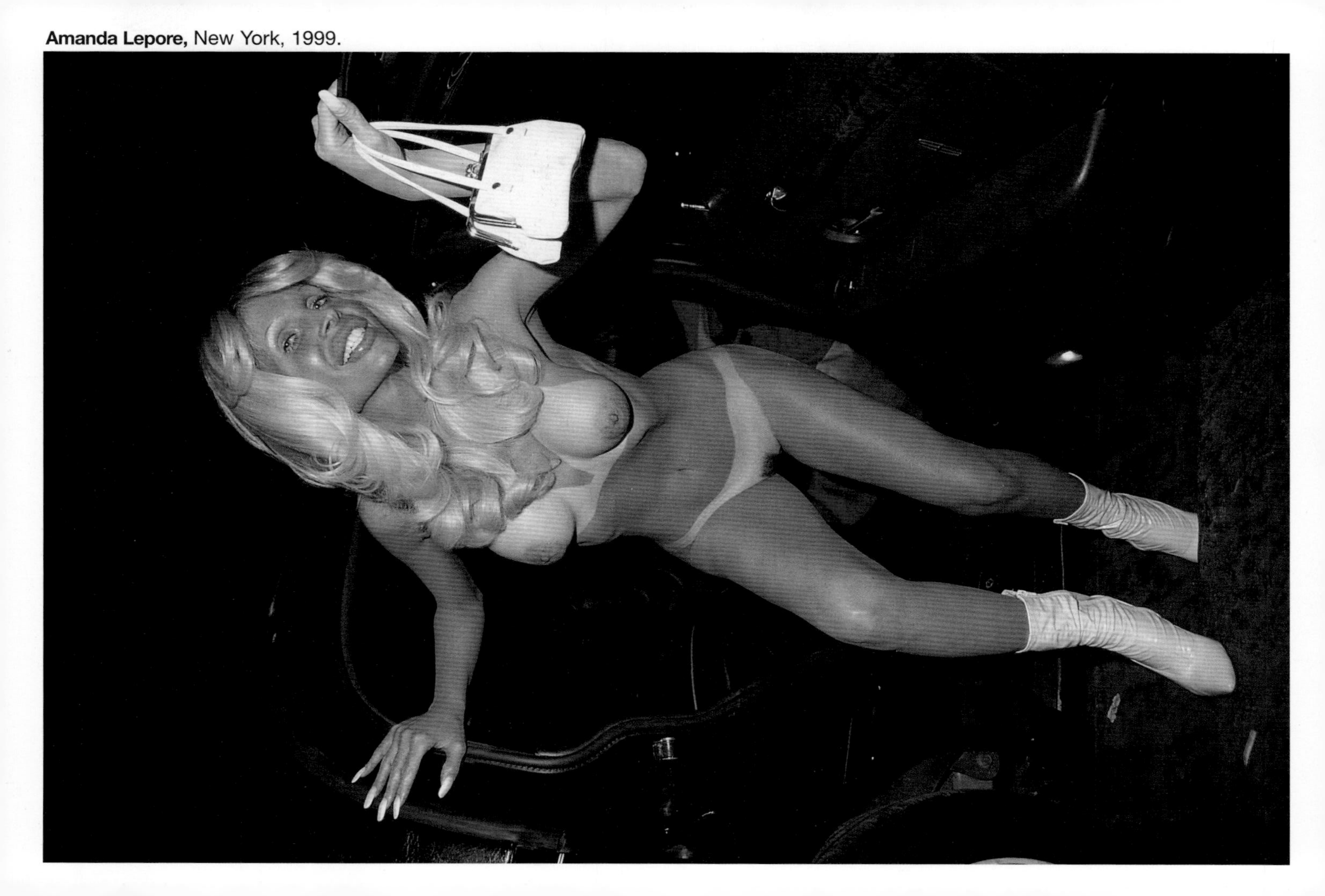

Latina Latuna, New York, 1978.

Bill Cunningham, New York, 1984.

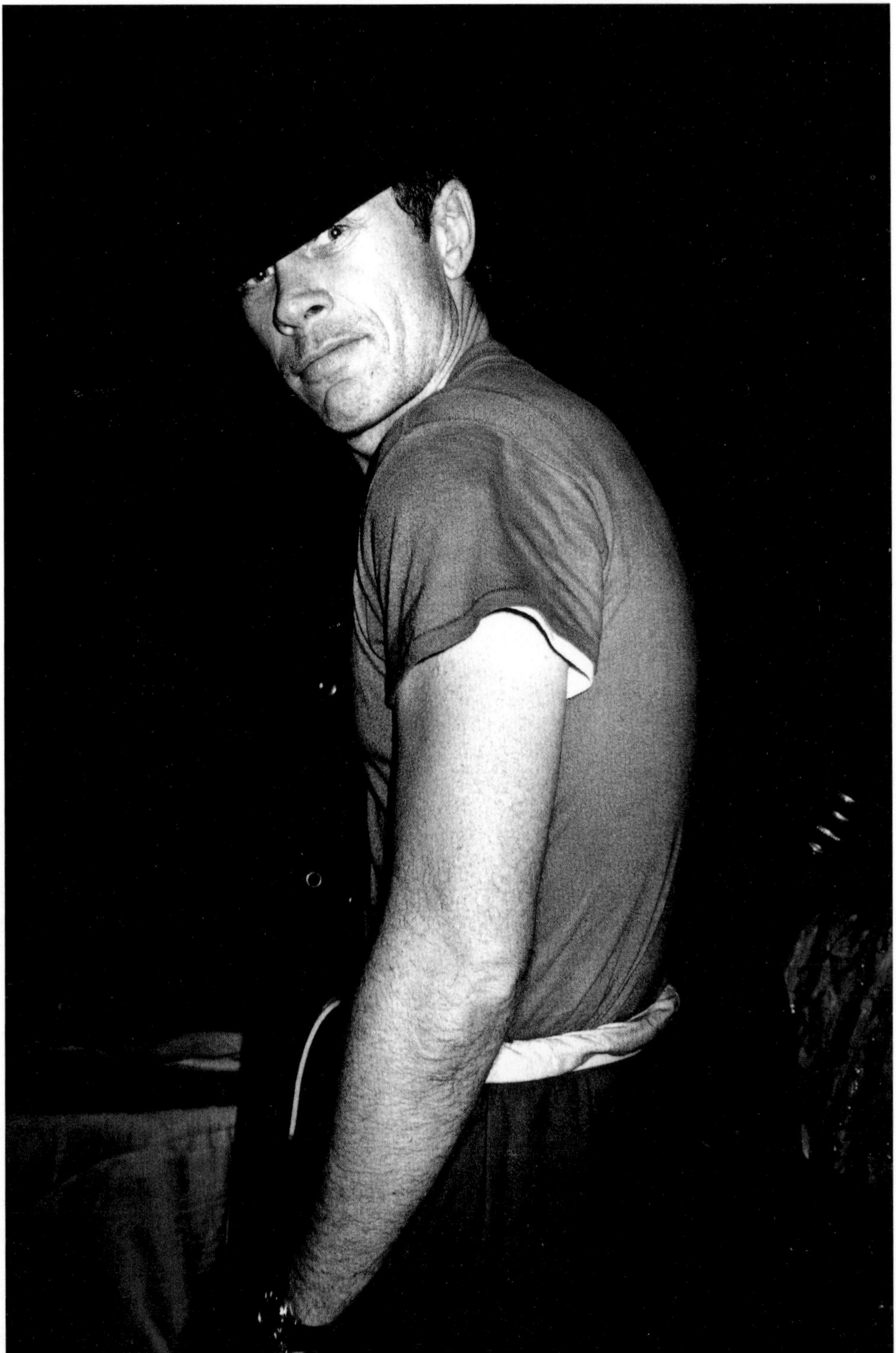

Jean-Paul Goude, Paris, 1981.

Mary Ellen Mark, New York, 1993.

Alexandre Assouline, Paris, 1997.

Partygoer, Paris, 1980.

Al Hirschfeld, New York, 1993.

Kenny Scharf, New York, 1995.

John F. Kennedy, Jr., New York, 1994.

john f. kennedy jr

The first time I ever met John F. Kennedy Jr. I asked him if I could take his picture. I was a bit shocked when he said, "Only if you can get me by surprise." I told him that I wasn't a paparazzi photographer: "I don't hide in the bushes. I get invited!" That made him laugh and after that I never had a problem taking his picture.

c.z. guest

(next page) I was very excited to be working with Polly Mellen on a big editorial shoot for *Allure* magazine: "All About Evening." We were using all the hot new girls—Chandra North, Carolyn Murphy—and the best gowns of the season by the biggest designers. Our setting was a star-studded benefit dinner. David Bowie and Iman, Iggy Pop, Coolio, Francesco and Alba Clemente were among an endless cast of characters. Carolyn was dressed and ready for action. We wanted to shoot her in a spot that gave off the energy of a fabulous party. Just then, Iggy Pop walked by and I grabbed him. At that same moment, C.Z. Guest stopped to say hello to me. I introduced C.Z. and Iggy (C.Z. had no idea who he was), and asked them if they would mind doing a picture with Carolyn for *Allure*. They willingly obliged and it made, not only a great photo, but Carolyn's night. Those are real emotions in the photo. She was thrilled to meet Mr. Pop.

C. Z. Guest, Iggy Pop, Carolyn Murphy, New York, 1995.

Hébé Dorsey, Jacqueline de Ribes, New York, 1984.

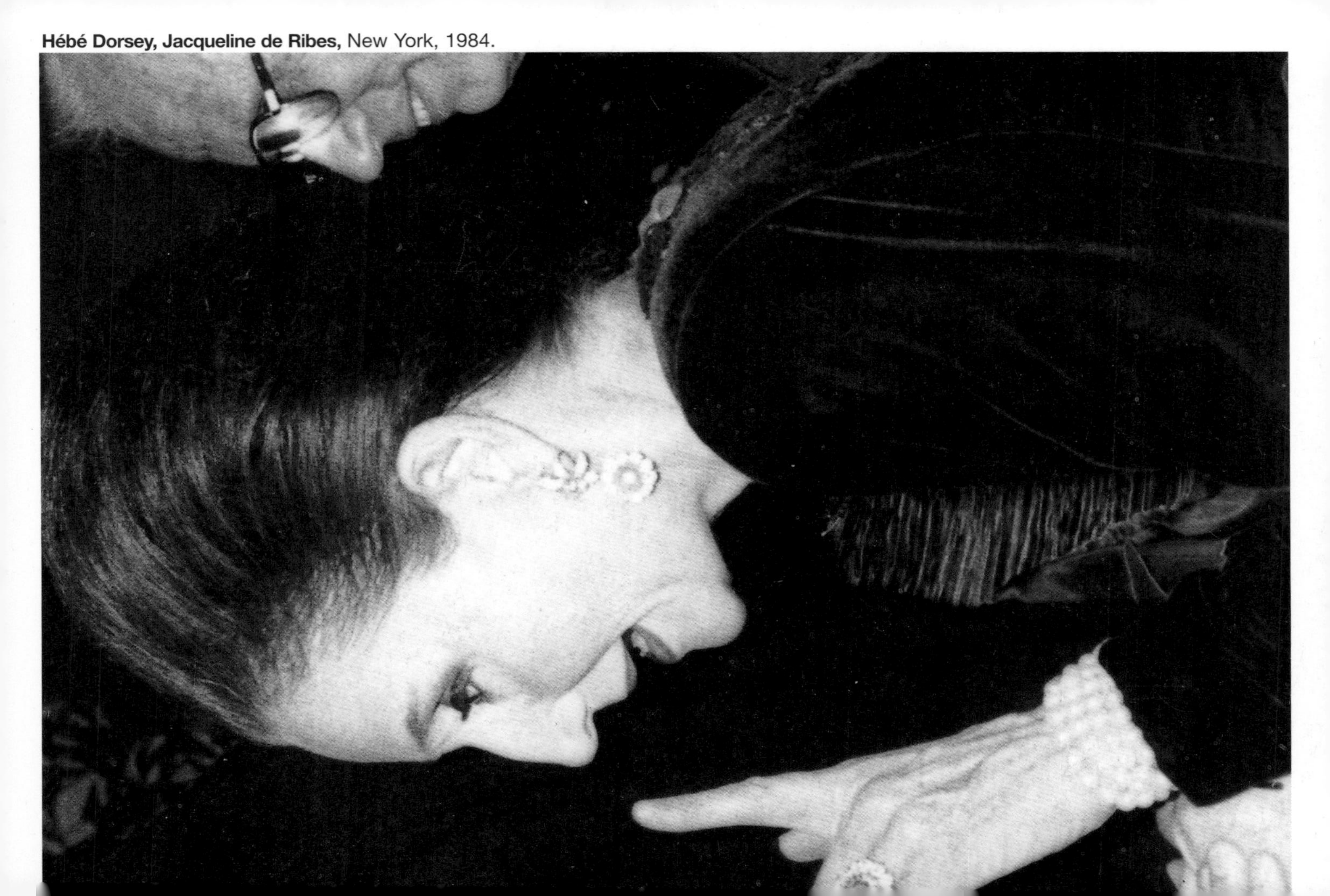

Liza Minnelli, Audrey Hepburn, New York, 1989.

Christian Lacroix, Carolyn Roehm, New York, 1988.

Erté, New York, 1992.

John Denver, Placido Domingo, Lionel Ritchie, New York, 1984.

Yves Saint Laurent, New York, 1983.

saint laurent

When Yves Saint Laurent was having a 25 year retrospective at the Metropolitan Museum of Art, I was his personal photographer. I covered every angle of the event as well as his stay in New York. When it was time for him to leave, I decided to go with him to the airport so I could get even more photos. They happened to have a mock-up of the Empire State Building at Barnes & Noble. I asked the manager if he thought I might be able to borrow it for a couple of hours so that I could take a photo of it with Yves Saint Laurent. He smiled as he opened up his blazer to show off the label inside that read "Yves Saint Laurent." Needless to say he let me borrow the mock-up, and, it made a great picture!

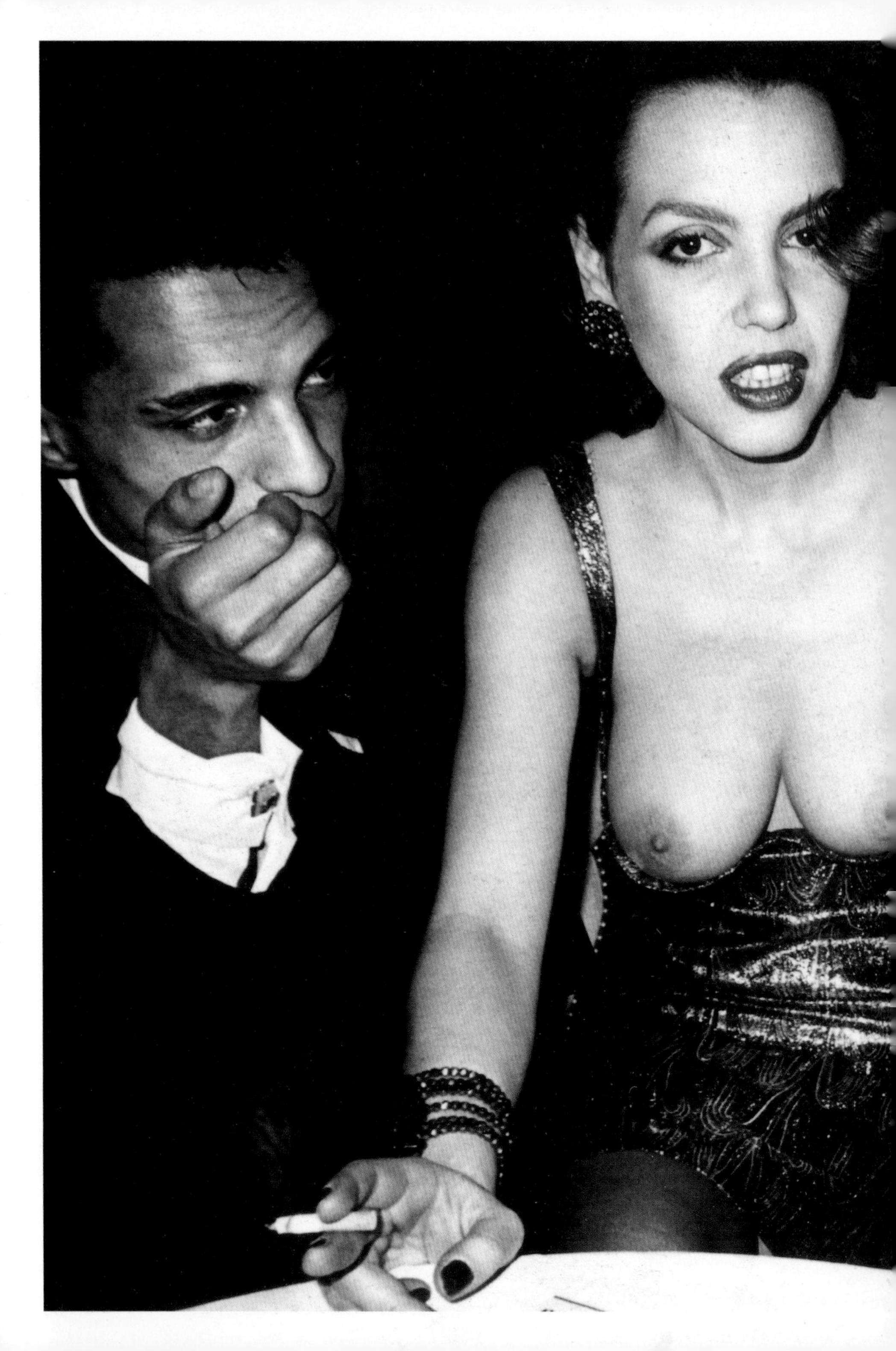

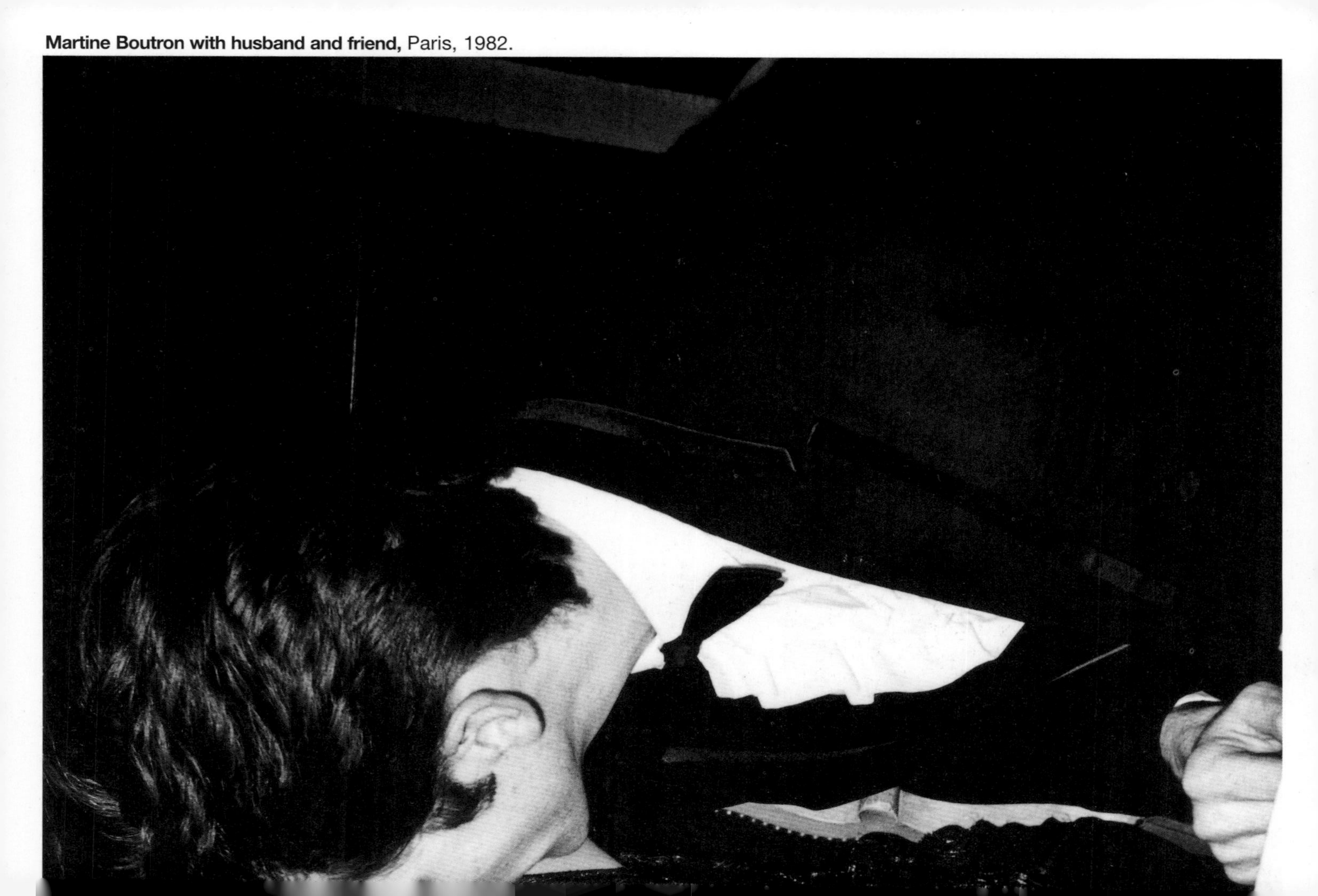

Martine Boutron with husband and friend, Paris, 1982.

Yves Saint Laurent, Diana Vreeland, New York, 1983.

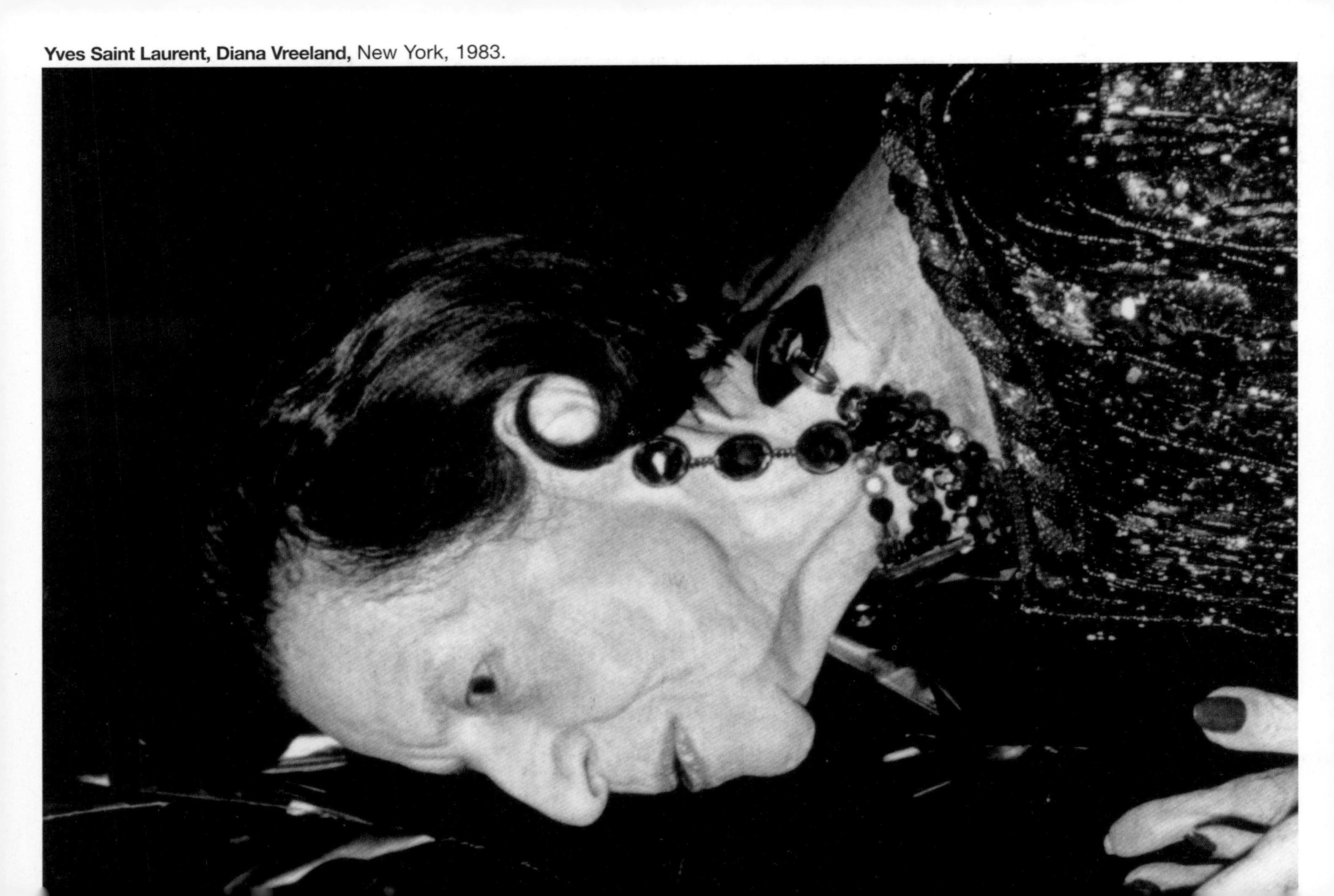

Richard Avedon, Milan, 1995.

Drew Barrymore, New York, 1992.

Hubert de Givenchy, Paris, 1980.

Halston, New York, 1979.

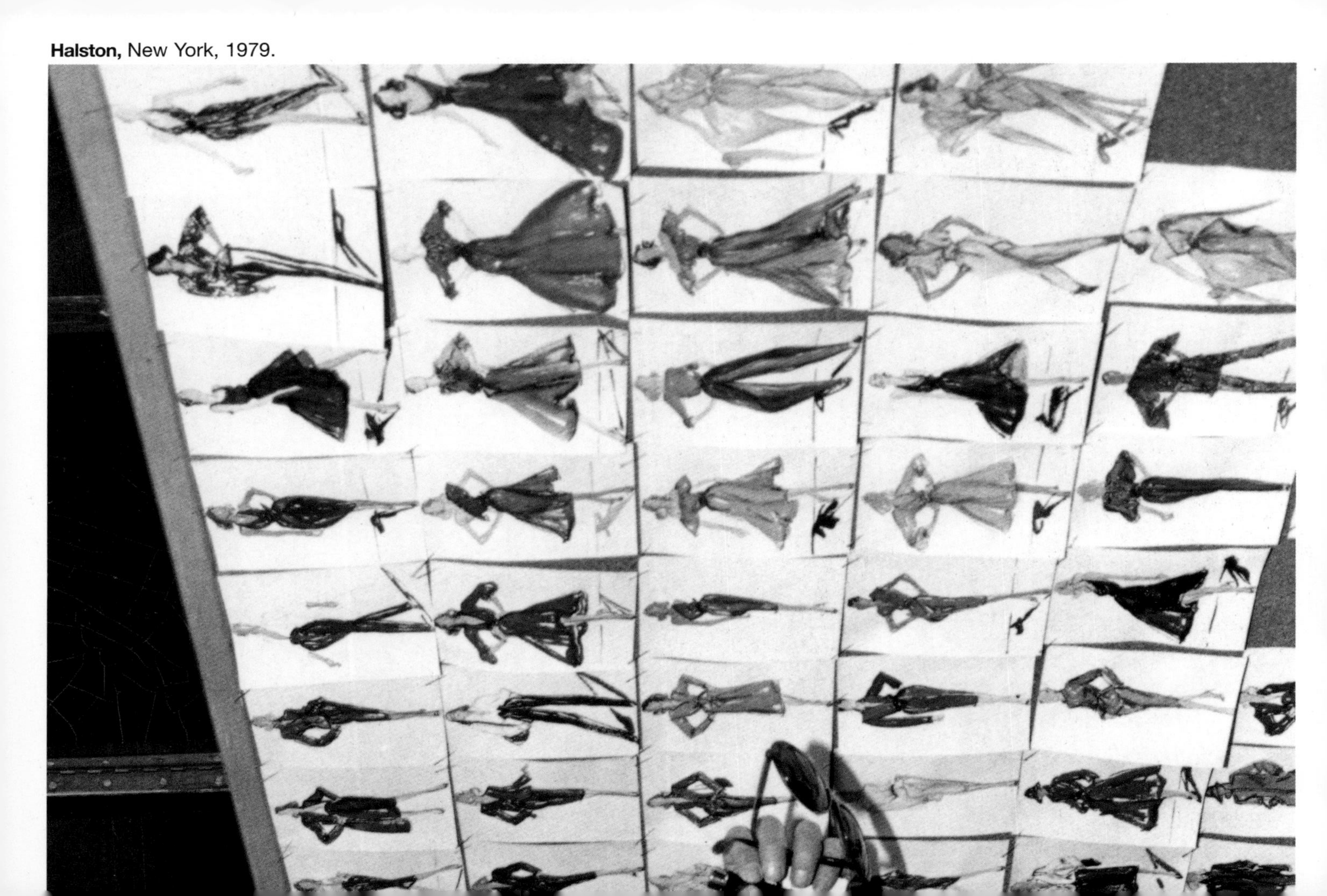

Pat Cleveland, New York, 1977.

pat cleveland

Of all the beautiful women and fabulous models I have worked with, there will never be another like Pat Cleveland. She took modeling to a whole new level. She was much more then a pretty face and a thin body. She was an interpreter. She would look in the mirror and decide how she needed to present herself. Her moods, attitude, walk and demeanor would change according to what she was wearing. In those days, models didn't just walk the runway looking straight ahead with one single expression on their faces, they would interact with the audience. Pat laughed, smiled, winked, danced, ran, jumped, cried—whatever was necessary. Once, at a Thierry Mugler show, Pat was wearing a gorgeous, corseted velvet gown. Madame Butterfly was playing as she minced down the long runway inch by inch. When she finally got to the end, she tilted her head back and pretended to take poison. Then collapsed right where she was standing. It was so full of drama! Everyone screamed and clapped, "Bravo, Bravo!" Then she managed to get off the floor by herself and walk back down the long runway with elegance and grace. At another show, Mugler had her suspended from a cable from the top of the cathedral-high ceiling, and slowly lowered her onto the runway. Her dress billowed around her as she floated down. She was dressed as the Virgin Mary, complete with halo and infant in her arms. No one could have pulled it off better. Another time, I don't recall the designer, Pat ran out on the runway and leapt flawlessly into the air, as if a prima ballerina. She didn't stop with just one, but leapt the entire length of the runway, soaring in the air above the audience.

Iman, Paris, 1983.

Grace Jones, New York, 1994.

Eubie Blake, Cab Calloway, Lionel Hampton, New York, 1980.

Barry White, New York, 1993.

James Brown, Paris, 1995.

Bobby Womack, New York, 1989.

Eva Ionesco, Paris, 1981.

Norman Mailer, New York, 1989.

Carmen Kass, Paris, 1998.

Steven Meisel, Christy Turlington, Herb Ritts, Naomi Campbell, New York, 1990.

Kristen McMenamy, Paris, 1997.

kristen mcmenamy

is a great model, subject and muse. She is full of personality, and lots of energy and drama! I have endless great moments of her. Her most remarkable quality is her determination and persistence. Kristen had already been modeling for years, but still she hadn't "made it." Anyone else would have given up. The odds were against her because all the other models were still going through puberty and Kristen was already in her mid-twenties. She took drastic measures when she shaved off her eyebrows. It worked. She got the attention and recognition she was looking for. Steven Meisel loved her and soon all the designers followed suit. She always had time for a photo, and gave it her all. She would do whatever it took to make a great photo, even if it meant taking all her clothes off. One time in the middle of fashion week in Europe, Kristen walked backstage with her arm in a sling. The night before, she was doing a photo shoot with her boyfriend Miles Aldridge. She was jumping on the bed for the photo and fell off and dislocated her shoulder. But she didn't let that interfere with her obligation to do all the shows. She stoically took off her sling and got on the runway, head held high, hiding her pain behind a smile.

Naomi Campbell, Christy Turlington, Linda Evangelista, Paris, 1990.

Shalom Harlow, Kristen McMenamy, Paris, 1997.

Sean Penn, Madonna, New York, 1999.

Canon

Gisele Bundchen, Milan, 2000.

Ivana Trump, Sandra Bernhard, Los Angeles, 1992.

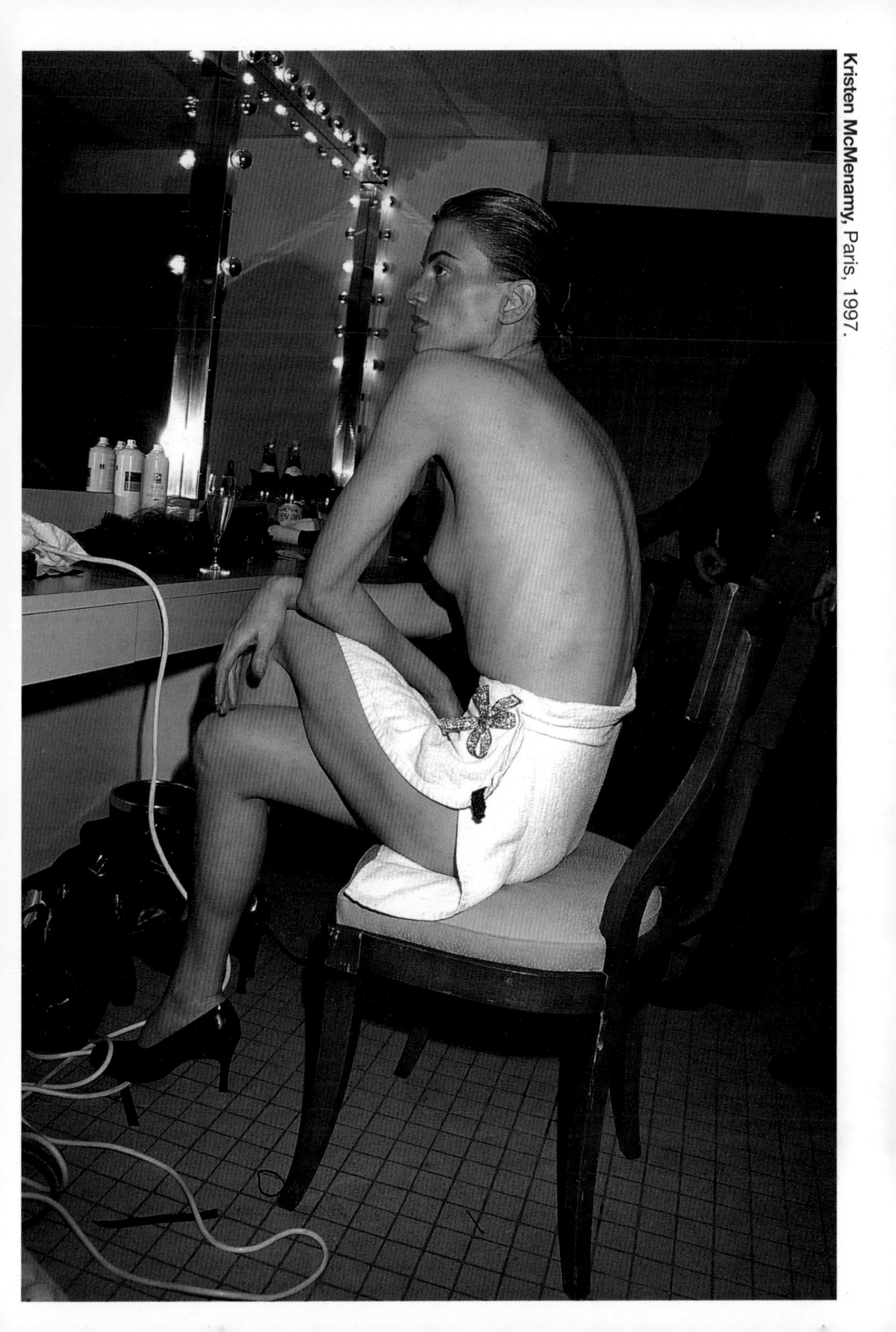

Kristen McMenamy, Paris, 1997.

Anne Slater, New York, 1992.

Linda Evangelista, Rome, 1991.

Amalia, Paris, 1999.

Kate Moss, Paris, 1996.

Amanda Lepore, New York, 1998.

amanda lepore

At the Azzedine Alaïa retrospective, David LaChapelle's muse, Amanda Lepore, showed up totally naked. When I introduced her to Azzedine, Amanda told him that since he didn't send her a dress she had nothing to wear. Most people that night didn't bat an eye at seeing her in the buff—probably because she usually isn't dressed and if she is, she's barely dressed at all.

Issey Miyake, Paris, 1980.

Vivienne Westwood, New York, 1994.

Halston, New York, 1978.

Yves Saint Laurent, New York, 1983.

Donatella Versace, Mickey Rourke, Miami, 1994.

Liza Minnelli, New York, 1980.

Elton John, New York, 1980.

Andy Warhol, Jacqueline Schnabel, Jean-Michel Basquiat, Julian Schnabel, Kenny Scharf, New York, 1984.

Roberto Benigni, New York, 1998.

roberto benigni

I was thrilled to be shooting Roberto Benigni for *Esquire*. *Johnny Stecchino* was one of my favorite movies, and I was really looking forward to meeting the man behind the laughter. When I arrived, he was eating lunch. "I am pleased to meet you," I said. "Con mucho gusto," he replied. "No, I am pleased to meet you." And we went back and forth like this for quite a while. He didn't want any makeup or anyone to do his hair. He didn't want us to adjust the seat on the bike for him. But when we were all ready, he hopped on the bike and with every click of the shutter there was another great photo, full of energy, expression and, above all, laughter.

David Bowie, Damien Hirst, Julian Schnabel, New York, 1996.

Italian ladies with dog, Milan, 1995.

Bono, Tony Shafrazi, Cap d'Antibes, 2000.

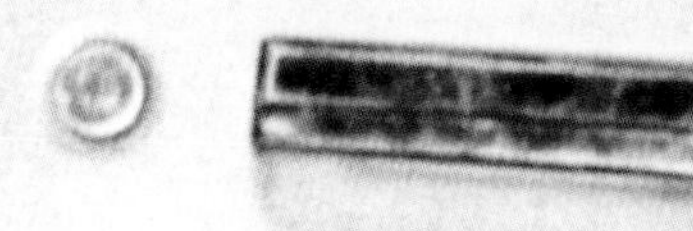

Sheryl Lee Ralph, Tom Eyen and friends, New York, 1987.

Paloma Picasso, Rafael Lopez Cambil, New York, 1982.

Stephan Weiss, Donna Karan, New York, 1991.

Mark Wahlberg, David Geffen, Los Angeles, 1992.

Gisele Bundchen, New York, 1997.

Masked men, London, 1997.

acknowledgments

To Vanessa Contessa Salle, my daughter, for loving me, supporting me, making me laugh, and your great eye. Thank you for all your writing. You are truly the best!

Jesse Frohman, I could not have done this book without your brilliant advice and incredible editing.

John Granito, thanks for ALWAYS being there for me, believing in me and for STILL letting me believe that life is a party.

To all my friends and "family," Jamie Cabreza, my assistant, who is always there to save me and Mike Cabreza, my printer, who spent so much time and effort to please me. Thank you.

Dede Hwang, my prize photo researcher, thanks for finding them and spelling everyone's name properly.

Heidi Hartwig, for your assistance in focusing the editing process.

Gabagh Kaghado, for finding lost causes in the madness.

Fritz Gruber, for your appreciation and caring which shows in your magnificent words.

Glenn O'Brien, for your ultra hip words and wit.

Dr. Brian Saltzman, for being such a special friend, who means so much to me.

Bill Regelson, for holding my hand and agonizing over the writing.

I love you all and couldn't have done it without your help, support and encouragement. Thanks.

To all the editors that I worked for and enabled me to capture many of these people. Tina Brown, Angelica Bleischmidt, Annie Flanders, Alexander Liberman, Anna Piaggi, Sally Singer, Franca Sozzani, Brittan Stone, Stefano Tonchi, Linda Wells, Anna Wintour, American Vogue, and Si Newhouse Jr., Condé Nast, thank you for your many years of support.

Thanks to everyone at Assouline, especially Martine and Prosper Assouline my publishers, for believing in me and making this dream come true.

But most of all, I am grateful to the countless, fascinating people who have inspired me throughout my career; the designers, models, artists, drag queens, partygoers, and everyone else who allowed me to capture their creative energy on film. Thank you.